That's Faith!

INSPIRING STORIES OF LATTER-DAY SAINTS
WHO TOOK THE LEAP OF FAITH

Timothy L Carver

Table of Contents

A Formula for Faith

"Even so faith, if it hath not works, is dead, being alone."[1]

Some time ago I came across a newspaper article that totally surprised me. It stated that more than 90% of Americans believe in God.[2] I wondered how so many people would claim to believe in God when there is so much crime, immorality, drug use and violence in this country. Furthermore, a recent Gallup poll showed that church attendance nationwide is dropping.[3] So how could 90% say they believe in God?

---

[1] James 2:17

[2] http://www.pewresearch.org/fact-tank/2018/04/25/key-findings-about-americans-belief-in-god/

[3] https://news.gallup.com/opinion/polling-matters/242015/church-leaders-declining-religious-service-attendance.aspx

Then I remembered something I had read by Elder James E. Talmage (1862 – 1933), a member of the Quorum of Twelve Apostles. He stated that belief and faith are *not* the same thing. A person can believe in something without living it. He went on to say that "faith implies such confidence and conviction as will impel to *action*."[4] In other words, belief can be idle and passive, while faith leads a person to *act* upon the teachings of Jesus Christ.

The Apostle James stressed this when he said to the mere believers of his day: "Thou believest that there is one God; thou doest well: the devils also believe and tremble. But wilt thou know, O vain man, that faith without works is dead?"[5]

Faith isn't faith unless we are *acting* upon our beliefs! We might write a simple formula for faith this way:

BELIEF + **ACTION** = THAT'S FAITH!

That's why faith in Jesus Christ is the *first* principle of the gospel. It's the principle that motivates us to *act* upon the Savior's teachings. And the greater the temptation or trial we experience, the greater the faith it takes to overcome it. Both Moroni and the apostle Peter describe these experiences as "the trial of faith".[6]

"Can I Measure My Faith?"

Several years ago one of my seminary students stayed after class to ask a question. Our lesson that day had been about faith and his question was this: "Is there any way I can measure how much faith I have?"

I thought it was a great question. I disappointed him a bit when I told him I didn't know of a way to actually gauge faith.

---

[4] *Articles of Faith*, 87

[5] James 2:19-20

[6] Ether 12:6, 1 Peter 1:7

2

But after pondering his question for several days I realized there is a way to measure faith. The apostle James taught that "faith, if it hath not works, is dead".[7] Faith is based on works. So we can measure our faith in Jesus Christ by measuring our obedience to His teachings.

I decided to prepare a lesson that would give my students an opportunity to gain insights into their level of faith. I gave each of them a list of commandments and guidelines the Lord has given us through His prophets – chastity, dating, tithing, and so on. As we discussed each commandment I shared a brief story of someone who, in a moment of trial, had exercised faith in that principle. The students were then given the opportunity to 'measure' their own faith by ranking from 1 to 10 how well they were *living* each of the teachings.

The impact of the lesson surprised me! Many students were significantly touched as they considered their faith in Jesus Christ.

Over the years I have shared this presentation in numerous classrooms and firesides. The positive impact has encouraged me to write a book that can hopefully share something of the same experience with readers. Each of the following chapters focuses on a commandment or principle the Lord has given us. The principle is then highlighted by a true story of someone who, in a moment of temptation or trial, took the leap of faith. Many of these people I knew personally and was privileged to have them share their story with me. In a few instances I actually knew of the trial they were experiencing and watched them pass the test of faith. I hope their stories will inspire you as they do me.

Here's a great story to start with.

"I'd Rather Follow What I Believe"

Aleisha Cramer Rose began playing soccer when she was 6 years old. At 16 she was playing on the U.S. women's national

---

[7] James 2:17

soccer team. She was later named the national high school player of the year and recruited by every national college soccer team. She finally settled on Brigham Young University (BYU) where Aleisha earned All-American honors each season and helped lead the Cougars to four straight NCAA Tournament appearances.

During her college years, she also played on the U.S. national team where her coach, April Heinrich, described Aleisha as, "The [most] impactful player in women's college soccer today. . . . She changed the game. At 19-years-of-age, that's about as good a compliment as you'll get from me without calling her the next Michael Jordan."[8]

She was in training for the 2003 World Cup and the 2004 Olympic soccer team when she stunned the soccer world by quitting the national team. Why? "There are games on Sundays," she said, "and I won't play on Sunday, no matter what."

That meant no more soccer tournaments in places like China, Italy, and Australia. No further opportunities for winning a gold medal.

Was the decision hard for her?

"If I had to do it over again I'd make the same decision. But when you make the right decisions it's still going to be hard. I was going to all these cool countries and now it's like I'm not going to do that anymore."[9]

Any regrets?

"Sure, it would be so awesome to be like Mia Hamm or Michelle Akers and represent your country – I loved those things. I guess

---

[8] https://byucougars.com/athlete/w-soccer/8029/Aleisha-Cramer%20Rose

[9] https://www.thechurchnews.com/archives/2002-11-30/she-quits-na-tional-team-stuns-soccer-world-105082

my standards are more important to me than being Mia Hamm. I'd rather follow what I believe."[10]

Belief + Action. That's faith!

---

[10] *Soccer America*, October 7, 2002, 14

1

Adversity

". . . know thou, my son, that all these things shall give thee experience, and shall be for thy good."[1]

Recently I came across a question someone posted on the internet: "What would the world be like today if Adam and Eve hadn't eaten that forbidden fruit?"

A minister of another faith had provided an answer stating that the fall of Adam and Eve was a huge mistake. He believed that God intended Adam and Eve (and their posterity) to live in a perfect world; one without sin or sorrow, death or temptation.

Latter-day scripture reveals that the Fall of Adam was, in fact, a part of our Father's plan and brought about changes needed

---

[1] Doctrine and Covenants 122:7

for our progression. After our first parents partook of the fruit the Lord stated:

> And unto Adam, I, the Lord God, said: Because thou hast hearkened unto the voice of thy wife, and hast eaten of the fruit of the tree of which I commanded thee, saying–Thou shalt not eat of it, cursed shall be the ground for thy sake. . .[2]

Did you catch that? The ground would be cursed for thy sake. The Lord then states that there would be thorns and thistles, trials and tribulations in this fallen world. These changes would grant us the opportunity of having experiences that would help us develop, grow and progress.

Adam and Eve later came to the realization that the Fall was a blessing for both them and their posterity:

> And in that day Adam blessed God and was filled, and began to prophesy concerning all the families of the earth, saying: Blessed be the name of God, for because of my transgression my eyes are opened, and in this life I shall have joy, and again in the flesh I shall see God.
>
> And Eve, his wife, heard all these things and was glad, saying: Were it not for our transgression we never should have had seed, and never should have known good and evil, and the joy of our redemption, and the eternal life which God giveth unto all the obedient.[3]

This earthly stage of our Father's plan was designed to give us challenges. Elder Orson F. Whitney (1855 – 1931), a member of the Twelve Apostles, stated:

> No pain that we suffer, no trial that we experience is wasted. It ministers to our education, to the development of such qualities as patience, faith, fortitude, and humility. All that we suffer and all that we

---

[2] Moses 4:23

[3] Moses 5:10-11

endure, especially when we endure it patiently, builds up our characters, purifies our hearts, expands our souls, and makes us more tender and charitable, more worthy to be called the children of God . . . and it is through sorrow and suffering, toil and tribulation, that we gain the education that we come here to acquire and which will make us more like our Father [in heaven].[4]

"If This Is What the Lord Wants"

I first met Paul Tingey while I was in the Language Training Mission (forerunner of the Missionary Training Center). He was an outstanding missionary. You rarely saw Elder Tingey without a smile on his face. His love, kindness, faith, and obedience soon led to leadership positions in our mission.

After returning from his mission Paul married and then graduated from the University of Utah, receiving his Bachelor of Arts degree in finance with honors. He later received an MBA degree. He was employed by IBM and Rolm, working in marketing and management. Not long afterward Paul was diagnosed with Multiple Sclerosis (MS), an unpredictable, disabling disease of the central nervous system that disturbs the flow of information between the brain and body.

Paul and I had lunch together a year or so after his diagnosis. We both ordered soup. I remember that because I watched how challenging it was for Paul to get each spoonful safely to his mouth without his shaking hand spilling it.

I asked about the disease and how it would progress. He told me that the symptoms and severity of MS vary from person to person. The disease can affect speech, eyesight, muscles and more. He said that it can take you quickly or can slowly rob you of ability and function.

I asked him how he felt about this trial in his life. I will never forget his answer. He looked me in the eyes and simply said, "Tim, if this is what the Lord wants, this is what I want." It was

---

[4] Quoted by Spencer W. Kimball in *Faith Precedes the Miracle* (1972), 98

a wonderful declaration of his faith in Jesus Christ. It was a powerful expression of his trust in the Lord's wisdom for the adversity He chooses to put in our path. His response reminded me of a scripture that both amazes and challenges me. The Lord promised that "he who receiveth all things with thankfulness shall be made glorious; and the things of this earth shall be added unto him, even an hundred fold, yea, more."[5]

What?! I'm supposed to be thankful when I get the flu? God wants me to be grateful when someone intentionally hurts or mocks me? Or when I've lost a loved one? I understand why I should be grateful for the good things but why would God want me to be thankful for the difficult things? And why the promise that those who are thankful in all things will be made glorious?

Elder Boyd K. Packer (1924 – 2015), a member of the Quorum of the Twelve Apostles, stated:

> It was meant to be that life would be a challenge. To suffer some anxiety, some depression, some disappointment, even some failure is normal. Teach our members that if they have a good, miserable day once in a while, or several in a row, to stand steady and face them. Things will straighten out. There is great purpose in our struggle in life.[6]

Paul Tingey patiently endured the effects of MS for more than 20 years. President Thomas S. Monson spoke of Paul in a Priesthood Session of General Conference:

> Just a month ago I attended [Paul Tingey's] funeral services here in Salt Lake City. Paul grew up in a fine Latter-day Saint home and served an honorable mission for the Lord in Germany. A companion of his in the mission field was Elder Bruce D. Porter of the First Quorum of the Seventy. Elder Porter described Elder

---

[5] Doctrine and Covenants 78:19

[6] *That All May Be Edified* [1982], 94

Tingey as one of the most dedicated and successful missionaries he ever knew.

At the conclusion of his mission, Elder Tingey returned home, completed his studies at the university, married his sweetheart, and together with her reared their family. He served as a bishop and was successful in his vocation.

Then, without much warning, the symptoms of a dreaded disease struck his nervous system—even multiple sclerosis. Held captive by this malady, Paul Tingey struggled valiantly but then was confined to a care facility for the remainder of his life. There he cheered up the sad and made everyone feel glad. Whenever I attended Church meetings there, Paul lifted my spirits, as he did all others.

When the World Olympics came to Salt Lake City in 2002, Paul was selected to carry the Olympic torch for a specified distance. When this was announced at the care facility, a cheer erupted from those patients assembled, and a hearty round of applause echoed through the halls. As I congratulated Paul, he said with his limited diction, "I hope I don't drop the torch!"

Brethren, Paul Tingey didn't drop the Olympic torch. What's more, he carried bravely the torch he was handed in life and did so to the day of his passing.

Spirituality, faith, determination, courage—Paul Tingey had them all.[7]

The Flames Will Not Hurt Thee

There is a purpose to the pain and trials we experience in this fallen world. Those who patiently exercise faith in the Father's plan and receive all things with thankfulness shall indeed "be made glorious".

---

[7] *Ensign*, May 2004

When through fiery trials thy pathway may lie,
My grace all sufficient shall be thy supply.
The flames will not hurt thee, my only design
Thy dross to consume and thy gold to refine.[8].

---

[8] "How Firm a Foundation," Hymns, no. 85

2

Baptism

"And the Father said, Repent ye, repent ye, and be baptized in the name of my Beloved Son."[1]

For those of us who were baptized at the age of eight, baptism was an exciting experience. But for many converts, it is a giant leap of faith. Many face opposition, leaving behind a former faith, friends, and family. Hopefully, these new members are soon swallowed up in new friendships that are formed as they become "no more strangers and foreigners, but fellow citizens with the saints, and of the household of God".[2]

The Lord clearly taught and repeatedly emphasized the importance of the ordinance of baptism in returning to the presence of our Heavenly Father:

---

[1] 2 Nephi 31:11

[2] Ephesians 2:19

Jesus answered and said unto him, Verily, verily, I say unto thee, Except a man be born again, he cannot see the kingdom of God.

Nicodemus saith unto him, How can a man be born when he is old? can he enter the second time into his mother's womb, and be born?

Jesus answered, Verily, verily, I say unto thee, Except a man be born of water and of the Spirit, he cannot enter into the kingdom of God.

That which is born of the flesh is flesh; and that which is born of the Spirit is spirit.

Marvel not that I said unto thee, Ye must be born again.[3]

Jesus not only set the example in being baptized[4], but both He and His apostles performed the ordinance of baptism for the faithful.[5] However, the power and authority to baptize were lost during the Great Apostasy.

In 1829 the resurrected John the Baptist laid his hands upon the heads of Joseph Smith and Oliver Cowdery and restored that same priesthood authority upon the earth.[6] What better messenger could Heavenly Father have sent down to restore this authority than the man who baptized Jesus?

This authority has been passed on to hundreds of thousands of faithful Elders so they are able to perform this ordinance of salvation throughout the world.

But some who investigate the Church wonder whether God would entrust this sacred power into the hands of such 'callow youth'. As a missionary in Germany from 1972 to 1974, I

---

[3] John 3:3-7

[4] Matthew 3:13-17

[5] JST John 4:1-4

[6] Doctrine and Covenants 13

witnessed several who had to pass that test of faith. One experience stands out to me.

Why Was She Weeping?

A woman from Spain was being taught by two missionaries in our district. I don't remember meeting this sister prior to the day of her baptism but I had often heard the missionaries speak of her. She was very receptive to the message of the Restoration and the missionaries loved teaching her.

Then came the time for the missionaries to challenge her to be baptized. Would she be willing to leave her former faith in order to accept this new religion? Could she accept the truth that these missionaries carried with them the power to act in the name of Jesus Christ? The missionaries were worried but hopeful. She was reading the Book of Mormon. She was attending church. And she was praying. All of these actions were demonstrating her faith in wanting to know of a surety that she was doing the right thing. When she was invited by the elders to accept a date for baptism, she accepted.

There weren't many baptisms in my mission during those times. We baptized about one person per missionary per year. So we were pleased when we learned that we were invited to attend the baptism.

Most of the details of the baptismal service have long since faded from memory. But there is one thing that took place that will forever stay with me. After the opening song and prayer, someone took a few minutes to give a talk regarding the importance of baptism. Then it was time for the baptisms to take place. There were several who were being baptized that day. When the young man ahead of her was being baptized I watched this sister put her head in her hands and begin to weep. My companion and I looked at each other and wondered if she had decided not to go through with the baptism.

But after the young man was helped from the baptismal font I watched this sister rise to her feet and make her way, without any hesitancy, into the baptismal font. She was baptized and came up with great joy radiating from her face.

We were confused. Why had she been weeping?

After the baptismal service, we stayed to chat with the two missionaries who had taught her. We had seen them talking to this sister after her baptism and wondered if she had told them what had brought her to tears. After she left we approached the missionaries.

"Did she tell you why she was crying?" we asked.

"Yes, she did," one of them quietly responded.

There was something about his response that told me that the answer was something very significant. Even sacred. I wasn't sure if I should ask my next question. But I did. "Can you share it with us?"

One of the Elders paused for a moment and then said, "She told us that she had her head bowed when the young man ahead of her stepped into the font. She looked up just as he was about to be baptized."

He paused, then continued.

"When she looked up she saw the young man who was being baptized. But it wasn't a missionary who was baptizing him. It was the Savior."

We all looked at each other in profound silence.

"That's when she began weeping," he said.

In His Name

Confirmation had been given to this woman that the authority to act in the name of Jesus Christ is back on the earth. It was a witness to her (and to us) that the baptismal ordinance performed by a worthy priesthood holder has the same validity as if done by the Savior Himself.

She had exercised her faith in Jesus Christ and she had been rewarded.

> And now, I, Moroni, would speak somewhat concerning these things; I would show unto the world that faith is things which are hoped for and not seen; wherefore, dispute not because ye see not, for ye receive no witness until after the trial of your faith.[7]

---

[7] Ether 12:6

3

Chastity

"Who shall ascend into the hill of the Lord? or who shall stand in his holy place? He that hath clean hands, and a pure heart."[1]

While serving as a bishop I had the responsibility to interview the teenagers in my ward at least once a year. One of the topics discussed in each interview was the law of chastity. I discovered that most of them understood that sexual relations prior to marriage is a serious sin. Most also understood why petting is a serious offense to the Lord. But many of them had a question. Some were brave enough to ask it, some were not. Their question was this: "How far can a person go in a relationship and still remain virtuous and clean? Where's 'the line'?"

---

[1] Psalms 24:3-4

I found if I could help them understand three important principles they could easily answer that question for themselves.

The Power of Procreation Is Good

First, I tried to help them understand that the power of procreation is a sacred gift from our Heavenly Father. Elder Boyd K. Packer (1924 – 2015), a member of the Quorum of the Twelve Apostles and President of the Quorum of the Twelve has taught:

> This power is good. It can create and sustain family life, and it is in family life that we find the fountains of happiness. It is given to virtually every individual who is born into mortality. It is a sacred and significant power, and I repeat, my young friends, that this power is good.
>
> Through the exercise of this power you can invite children to live with you—little boys and little girls who will be your very own—created, in a way, in your own image. You can establish a home, a dominion of power and influence and opportunity. This carries with it great responsibility."[2]

Passions Have One Proper Place

After emphasizing that this power is good and from our Heavenly Father, I would take a sheet of paper and draw a line down the middle of it. At the top of the paper on the left side I would write the word "Dating". At the top on the right side, I would write "Marriage". Under the "Dating" column I would ask the young person to list all of the purposes of dating. He or she would write down things such as:

- Discovering things you like in a future companion

- Helping you find a future companion

---

[2] *Ensign,* July 1972

- Getting to know other people

- Learning social skills

- Having fun

Then I would ask them to list the purposes of marriage. Under the "Marriage" column the typical responses would be:

- Having an eternal companion

- Bringing children into the world

- Fulfilling a requirement for eternal life

I then would ask, "Do you see anything on the marriage side of the line that involves passion and the power of procreation?" Their answer was always, "Yes."

My final question was, "Do you see anything on the dating side of the line that requires the use of passion and the creative power?" Their answer was always, "No."

Then I would point to the line between the two columns and say, "When you do anything on a date that causes your passions to be aroused, you've crossed the line. You've gone too far. You've begun tampering with a sacred gift that is designed to be used only in marriage."

Passions Are Powerful

Finally, I wanted to help them understand how powerful passions can be. Alma compares our passions to a horse. Anyone who has ridden a horse knows that the horse is much stronger than the rider. So a rider uses a bridle to control and guide the horse. Alma counseled his son Shiblon to "bridle" his passions.[3] Unbridled passions, like unbridled horses, are very difficult to control.

Satan seeks to persuade us to toy with our passions. He tries to convince us that there is no harm in necking, passionate

---

[3] Alma 38:12

kissing, French kissing, body massages, and other things that stimulate the passions. He knows that aroused passions can become overpowering. Young people who never considered being involved in sexual relations can quickly find themselves pulled in by the power of their passions. As a bishop, I have interviewed several people who told me that they never imagined they would ever be sitting across a desk from a bishop and confessing a sin of immorality. When I asked them what they thought led up to the sin, the explanation was always the same. They had been involved in repeated experiences that aroused their passions. Until the passions finally took over.

"No One Told Me"

A close friend named Gary shared an experience with me I have never forgotten. He had been talking with a friend of his who is a Latter-day Saint and also a family physician. His friend had seemed a little depressed so Gary asked, "What's up? You seem quieter than usual."

"Not a fun day at work," he said. Gary sensed that his friend needed to talk so he waited and listened.

After a moment the doctor continued. "I want you to visualize in your mind the most outstanding young woman in your stake. This would be a girl who is very active, careful who she dates, modest in her dress and has her eyes on the temple. Can you think of someone in your stake like that."

"Sure," Gary said.

"Well, I had a young woman like that in my office today. And I had to tell her that she was pregnant. When I told her, she began sobbing and repeatedly saying, 'It's not fair. No one told me.'

"I finally asked her what she meant by that. Through her tears, she responded, 'No one ever told me that your passions can be so powerful that you can't stop.'"

A Prophet's Warning

President Spencer W. Kimball (1895 – 1985), twelfth president of the Church, gave a strong warning to those who toy with their passions:

> Immorality does not begin in adultery or perversion. It begins with little indiscretions like sex thoughts, sex discussions, passionate kissing, petting and such, growing with every exercise. The small indiscretion seems powerless compared to the sturdy body, the strong mind, the sweet spirit of youth who give way to the first temptation. But soon the strong has become weak, the master the slave, spiritual growth curtailed. But if the first unrighteous act is never given root, the tree will grow to beautiful maturity and the youthful life will grow toward God, our Father.[4]

"Why I'm Proud of My Son"

Those who are wise do not involve themselves in any activity that promotes passion. An excellent example of this was shared with me by one of my friends. He approached me at work one day and asked, "Hey, is it okay if I brag about one of my sons?"

"Sure, dads are supposed to brag about their children," I said, smiling.

"Well, two of my boys play on the high school basketball team. Last Friday night we were playing our cross-town rivals. They're a bigger school and we rarely beat those guys. But with about 15 seconds left the game was tied. They got the ball to my son, Justin. He took an outside jump shot, scored the hoop and won the game. He was the hero."

"That's awesome!" I said.

Then he surprised me. "But that isn't what I wanted to brag about. It's what happened *after* the game."

---

[4] *Ensign*, November 1980

Now I was really curious. "So what happened after the game?"

"After every game, my wife and I always go back to our house, dish up some ice cream, sit around the table and talk about the game with our two sons. While we were talking the phone rang and Justin was called to the phone. He answered it, talked quietly for a few seconds, then hung up. It was a little odd, so when he came back to the table I asked him who was on the phone. He shook his head and said, 'It was no one, Dad.'

"That made me more curious so I asked again, 'Who was on the phone, Justin?'

"'I don't know who it was, Dad. She said she was a cheerleader for the other team. She told me I looked all sexy in my basketball shorts. She wanted to know if I wanted to meet her somewhere tonight.'

"I asked, 'So what did you tell her?'

"He looked at me and said, 'I told her I'm not interested in that kind of stuff and I hung up.'

My friend looked at me and smiled. "That's why I'm proud of my son," he said.

The Joy of Personal Purity

It probably wouldn't surprise you to know that Justin served a faithful mission. Nor would it surprise you to know he is now married in the temple and raising a wonderful family with his eternal companion. Justin's faith in following the Lord's counsel kept the passions at a distance and led him to the joy and peace of personal purity.

4

Dating

*"The Lord has made us attractive one to another for a
great purpose. But this very attraction becomes as a
powder keg unless it is kept under control."*
- President Gordon B. Hinckley[1]

When I was about 10 years old my brothers and I were excited to learn that a reservoir was going to be dug about a block from our house. Huge machinery was brought in to dig the hole. Over a period of weeks we watched the reservoir take shape as dirt was removed and the sides were sloped. We watched as the workers used large hoses to spray concrete onto the walls of the reservoir. We were excited because we knew the best part was coming – the water! We were going to have a swimming pool a block from our house!

---

[1] *Ensign*, January 2001

Our hopes were dashed when we saw the workers installing an 8-foot chain link fence around the reservoir. And along the top of the fence they put barbed wire. Then they filled it with water. We were not happy! No swimming pool for the Carver boys!

A couple of weeks later I was in the kitchen when my dad came home from work. I heard him tell my mother that two of my brothers had been seen sitting at the edge of the reservoir dangling their feet into the water. My brothers later told me that they had found a gap below the fence and had crawled underneath.

I still remember my mother's eyes filling with tears as she realized the danger my brothers had been in. Had they slipped into the water it would have been very difficult for them to get back out. The sides were sloped and there were no handholds.

So how did my brothers and I feel about the fence? To us it was a barrier to having some fun. How did my parents feel? To them it was a protection against serious danger.

The Lord's Fences

In the dating years, teens may feel the same about the Lord's dating guidelines as we felt about the fence – barriers to having some fun. But those who are wise realize the Lord's guidelines always provide protection to the obedient.

Here are some dating safety guidelines the leaders of the Church have given us:

1. Don't date until you are at least 16.

2. Date people with high standards.

3. Honor the sanctity of the priesthood and womanhood.

4. Avoid going on frequent dates with the same person.

5. Date in groups.

6. Let parents meet those you date.

7. Never be alone with a date in a home or bedroom.

8. Wear modest clothing.

9. Say a personal prayer before going on a date.[2]

Elder Boyd K. Packer (1924 – 2015), a member of the Quorum of the Twelve Apostles counseled:

> How foolish is the youth who feels that the Church is a fence around love to keep him out. Oh, youth, if you could know! The requirements of the Church are the highway to love and to happiness, with guardrails securely in place, with guideposts plainly marked, and with help along the way.
>
> How unfortunate to resent counsel and restraint. How fortunate are you who follow the standards of the Church, even if just from sheer obedience or habit. You will find a rapture and a joy fulfilled.[3]

We Both Need to Exercise Faith

Several years ago I had the opportunity to speak at a stake youth conference on the topic of faith. We talked about many guidelines listed in *For the Strength of Youth* including the Lord's counsel on dating. We discussed how faith is required to follow that counsel.

Several weeks later I was approached by a woman who asked, "Do you remember speaking at the youth conference in our stake?"

"Sure."

"Would you like some feedback on one of the girls who attended?"

"Absolutely."

---

[2] *For the Strength of Youth*, Dating

[3] *New Era*, June 2004

She then told me that this young lady had been steady dating a young man in her high school. She liked him. He liked her. But during that fireside the Spirit spoke to her heart. She realized that her steady dating was not following the Lord's counsel. She prayed about it and decided she wanted to exercise faith in what He was asking of her.

She went to her boyfriend and told him she still wanted to be friends but no longer wanted to steady date. He tried to talk her out of her decision.

"Look," he said, "We like each other. We like being with each other. And we're being good."

"But we're not following the Lord's counsel," she said.

With tears in his eyes, he pleaded with her to change her mind. She gently told him, "We both need to exercise faith by obeying what the Lord is asking us to do."

Faith in His Fences

This young woman did a difficult thing. Was it what she *wanted* to do? No. But she trusted in the Lord's promises that she would be safer and happier if she followed His counsel. *That's faith!*

5

Family History

"And he shall plant in the hearts of the children the promises made to the fathers, and the hearts of the children shall turn to their fathers. If it were not so, the whole earth would be utterly wasted at his coming."[1]

Several years ago I came across a journal account written by a man named Frederick W. Hurst. He was one of the workers who helped to paint the interior of the Salt Lake Temple prior to its dedication in 1893. In his journal he shared a sacred experience that has helped me better understand the reality of the Spirit World and how anxious our ancestors are to have their work done.

---

[1] Doctrine and Covenants 2:2-3

I Have Come From the Spirit World

"In the fall and winter of 1892-3, I worked at painting in the Salt Lake Temple. Although sick, I felt strongly impressed to go and do my very best.

"At noon the third day after beginning, President [Wilford] Woodruff called all the workmen together. He said he had been told that some of the workmen had stated that it would be impossible to have the temple completed by April 6. He said when he looked at this body of men, he didn't believe a word of it. 'Some of you may be sick and weak' (I thought he was talking to me), he continued. 'Some of you may give out at night, but you will be here in the morning if you are faithful. You are not here by accident; you were ordained in the eternal world to perform this work. Brethren, I will be here April 6th to dedicate this building. I know what I am talking about, for this was shown me in a vision fifty years ago in the city of Boston.'

"At times during that winter I was so sick with vomiting I dare not ride on a street car. I had two miles to walk to my lodging at Creighton Hawkins' home, which was located in the First Ward. Often the Brethren would say to me, 'You can't go to work tomorrow.' I thought of President Woodruff's promise and didn't miss a day all winter but was constant until the work was finished.

"Along about the 1st of March, 1893, I found myself alone in the dining room; all had gone to bed. I was sitting at the table when to my great surprise my elder brother Alfred walked in and sat down opposite me at the table and smiled. I said to him (he looked so natural): 'When did you arrive in Utah?'

"He said, 'I have just come from the spirit world; this is not my body that you see; it is lying in the tomb. I want to tell you that when you were on your mission you told me many things about the Gospel, and the hereafter, and about the spirit world being as real and tangible as the earth. I could not believe you, but when I died and went there and saw for myself, I realized that you had told the truth. I attended the Mormon meetings.'

"He raised his hand and said with much warmth, 'I believe in the Lord Jesus Christ with all my heart. I believe in faith, and repentance, and baptism for the remission of sins, but that is as far as I can go. I look to you to do the work for me in the temple.'

"He continued: 'You can go to any kind of sectarian meeting in the spirit world. All our kindred there knew when you were trying to make up your mind to come and work on the Temple. You are watched closely, every move you make is known there, and we are glad you came. We are all looking to you as our head in this great work. I want to tell you that there are a great many spirits who weep and mourn because they have relatives in the Church here who are careless and are doing nothing for them.'

"Three different times during our conversation I leaned over the table towards him and said, 'Alfred, you look, talk, and act perfectly natural: it doesn't seem possible that you are dead.'

"And every time he replied. 'It is just my spirit you see; my body is in the grave.'

"There was a great deal more that he told me, but these are the important items as I remember them. He arose and went out through the door that he had entered.

"As I sat pondering upon what I had seen and heard, with my heart filled with thanks and gratitude to God, the door opened again, and my brother Alexander walked in and sat down in the chair that Alfred had occupied. He had died in 1852 in New Zealand. I did the work for both him and Father in April 1885. He had come from a different sphere; he looked more like an angel, as his countenance was beautiful to look upon.

"With a very pleasant smile he said: 'Fred, I have come to thank you for doing my work for me, but you did not go quite far enough,' and he paused. Suddenly it was shown to me in large characters. 'NO MAN WITHOUT THE WOMAN, AND NO WOMAN WITHOUT THE MAN IN THE LORD.'

"I looked at him and said, 'I think I understand; you want [your wife] sealed to you.'

"He said, 'You are right—I don't need to interpret the scriptures to you, but until that work is done, I cannot advance another step.'

"I replied that the Temple would be completed and dedicated in about four weeks and then I would attend to it as quickly as possible.

"'I know you will,' he said, and then got up and left the room, leaving me full of joy, peace, and happiness beyond description."[2]

All Should Be Engaged

I am one who has long been guilty of thinking, "I'll start working on my family history when I'm old and retired. I don't have time for that now." Elder David A. Bednar, of the Quorum of the Twelve Apostles, has taken that excuse from me:

> Many of you may think family history work is to be performed primarily by older people. But I know of no age limit described in the scriptures or guidelines announced by Church leaders restricting this important service to mature adults. You are sons and daughters of God, children of the covenant, and builders of the kingdom. You need not wait until you reach an arbitrary age to fulfill your responsibility to assist in the work of salvation for the human family.[3]

I continued, however, to justify my lack of effort in doing family history by pointing out that I am still working a job and also have several callings in my ward. Then I came across a comment by President Henry B. Eyring in which he talked about working on his own family history. The Spirit spoke to my heart: "Do you think you're busier than President Eyring? If a member of the First Presidency has found time to work on family history, can't you?"

---

[2] *Diary of Frederick William Hurst*, comp. Samuel H. and Ida Hurst [1961]

[3] General Conference, October 2011

I decided to repent! Thanks to some wonderful members in my ward I began the adventure of "treasure hunting" in my own family history. And it wasn't long before I "struck gold".

A Precious Journal

In my initial searching, I came across a journal written by my great-great-grandfather, John Carver. He was born August 6, 1822, at Clifford Parish, Herefordshire, England. Baptized into the Church of Jesus Christ of Latter-day Saints in May of 1842, John later moved to South Wales where he could participate in organized branches of the Church. In 1847 he was ordained an Elder and was called to return to his homeland where he served as a missionary for three years.

Throughout the time of his missionary service, he and his fellow missionaries stayed in the home of James Eames. During that time all the members of the Eames family joined the Church except the daughter Mary Ann. John boldly told her, "I'll baptize you within the month." To prove him wrong she joined the Methodist faith but was quickly disfellowshipped a week later for dancing! John did baptize her and would marry her during their 1850 immigration voyage to America.

This is his journal account of the day he married his sweetheart (original spelling and punctuation preserved):

> This day (10th) will be a day long to be remembered to me. At an erly ower [early hour] I prepared for to fulfill that which God has required of every man that is to take to themselves a pardner in life and ever able to support her. Thereafter at about 11 o'clock A.M. myself and Miss Mary Ann Eames present owerselves before Elder Thomas Day to enter into covenant together as man and wife according to the order of the Kingdom of God. It will be remembered that owing to the high toss of the sea and the rocking of the ship caused us to be held up

by Elder Chel Evans (of Lehi Utah) as we was unable to stand."[4]

Three Years in the Mines

It took eight weeks to reach New Orleans. From there they traveled to St. Louis where John worked in a coal mine to earn money for the journey to Utah. During this time Mary Ann gave birth to two little boys, the oldest of whom died. In April 1853, three years after arriving in St. Louis, they continued their journey west.

They traveled to Iowa where they purchased a handcart. Then John and his little family began their five-month walk to the Salt Lake Valley, arriving in September of 1853. They would eventually become some of the initial settlers in Plain City, a community in northern Utah. John became a counselor to the Presiding Elder of Plain City and later became the Presiding Elder.

A Messenger from God

While serving in the Plain City Branch, John found himself facing a major decision. A gold mine was said to have been found at Little Mountain. Many of the men left their homes and families in search of possible treasure. My great-great-grandfather struggled to know what he should do. This was a time of great poverty for him and many of his fellow Saints. Finding gold would mean improving the struggling situation of his family. But this was also a time in which a smallpox epidemic had taken hold of their community. Many were sick and dying. He deeply feared that the dreaded "pox" would take hold of his family while he was gone. His solution was to do what he had always done. He would ask God. And God would answer him.

In his journal, John recorded that he was caught up in a vision in which a "Messenger took me to Little Mountain to convince

---

[4] *The Family of John Carver*, 1822-1912, published by the John Carver Family Organization

me. 'See,' said the Messenger, 'there is nothing here, only the upheaving of the earth. You will see these men come home broke and their families will suffer because of their greed for gold. Care for the sick in Plain City, and all will be well with you.'"[5]

John's question had been answered. He exercised his faith and stayed behind. He cared for the sick, built coffins and buried those who had died. And he quietly watched as the words of the messenger were fulfilled. All who had gone in search of gold returned empty-handed and sorrowing.

A Treasure Found

My great-great-grandfather never found any treasure of gold. But His faith in Jesus Christ led him to much greater treasures. And in exercising my faith to begin my family history I am also finding treasures. And they are turning my heart to my fathers.

---

[5] Ibid.

6

Forgiving Others

*"I, the Lord, will forgive whom I will forgive, but of you
it is required to forgive all men."*[1]

I never knew either of my grandfathers. Both passed away before I was born. While growing up I would occasionally hear stories about my dad's father. But I don't remember hearing stories about my mother's father. I hadn't even seen a photo of him until fairly recently. Not until I was an adult did I learn why he was never talked about in our home.

He was born in Hooper, Utah in 1887. At the age of 21, he married my grandmother. He was a hard-working man whose labor in road construction often took him away from home for long periods of time. That may have been one of the reasons my grandfather and grandmother struggled in their relationship.

---

[1] Doctrine and Covenants 64:10

After the birth of seven children, they divorced. My grandfather remarried and rarely visited his family.

My mother was the youngest child. She grew up during the Depression Era – hard times for our nation. Everyone went without a lot of things. But going without a father and a breadwinner made things especially difficult. My grandmother picked up odd jobs and the older children worked hard to help provide basic needs.

My mother rarely spoke of the difficulty of those days. But she did tell me she remembered her mother occasionally saying, "I don't think I'm going to eat supper tonight. I'm not very hungry." It wasn't until she got older that she realized her mother was skipping the meal because there wasn't enough. "I'm sure she was just as hungry as the rest of us," my mother told me. "She would skip dinner to make sure her children had enough to eat."

In the meantime, my grandfather was not suffering. He still had a job and was making good money. Yet rarely was any of it passed on to his family. My mother recalled once receiving 50 cents from her father on her birthday. She couldn't remember receiving any other gift from him.

The more I learned about my grandfather the more I developed a quiet resentment toward him. I felt a deep desire to stand toe to toe with him and tell him what I thought of a man who would ignore his family, especially in times of great need.

Life's Too Short for Grudges

Then something happened that changed all that. It took place at my mother's 80th birthday celebration. We had enjoyed a quiet get-together with close family members. After dinner, we watched a fun slide presentation showing photos of my mother from the time she was a little girl until she was married. There were also photos of my grandmother and my mother's siblings but there were no photos of my grandfather.

Then one of my brothers spoke up. "Didn't your father take off and leave the family when you were little?"

My mother paused and gently said, "I forgave my father a long time ago. Life's too short to hold grudges. I've been blessed with a good life."

As she said those words the Spirit spoke clearly to my heart: "Your mother has forgiven your grandfather. Why haven't you?"

As I pondered that piercing impression I was reminded that unless I could forgive my grandfather for his failures and weaknesses I was petitioning in vain for the Lord to forgive mine. I decided it was time to forgive my grandfather. And I have.

A Lesson on Forgiving

Not long after that, I had an experience that helped me realize I was not the only one struggling to forgive someone. It came during a lesson I was teaching to my seminary students about forgiving others. We were reading the Lord's requirement of forgiving those who have wronged us if we are to have our own sins forgiven:

> My disciples, in days of old, sought occasion against one another and forgave not one another in their hearts; and for this evil they were afflicted and sorely chastened.
>
> Wherefore, I say unto you, that ye ought to forgive one another; for he that forgiveth not his brother his trespasses standeth condemned before the Lord; for there remaineth in him the greater sin.
>
> I, the Lord, will forgive whom I will forgive, but of you it is required to forgive all men.[2]

I confessed to my students that forgiving others is not something that is particularly easy for me. I told them that I had been struggling with some resentful feelings toward my grandfather.

---

[2] Doctrine and Covenants 64:8-10

Then came an impression. It made me a bit nervous but I decided to exercise faith and follow the prompting. I said, "I'm going to ask each of you, one by one, if there is anyone in your life you resent, hold a grudge against or are struggling to forgive. I don't want any names or any details. I just want you to look in your heart, then look me in the eyes and answer yes or no."

The results surprised me. I think it surprised everyone in the class. As I called upon each student, the overwhelming majority of them quietly admitted that they were struggling to forgive someone. There were a few who were able to sincerely say, "I can't think of anyone I haven't forgiven." But most were experiencing some level of difficulty in forgiving someone who had offended or hurt them.

I repeated that question in every class that day. The results were the same. Nearly every student in every class was struggling to forgive at least one person.

I am convinced that the Lord's requirement to forgive others is something that not only teens struggle with. And I believe that for many of us this is one of the most difficult of the Lord's teachings to follow.

Afflicted in Any Manner

So how does a person find the ability to fully and forever forgive? And not just those who are easy to forgive. But even those who intentionally and repeatedly hurt us.

We are not expected to do it alone. During His visit to the Nephites, the Lord extended a powerful invitation to the people: "Have ye any that are sick among you? Bring them hither. Have ye any that are lame, or blind, or halt, or maimed, or that are deaf, *or that are afflicted in any manner*? Bring them hither and I will heal them."[3]

---

[3] 3 Nephi 17:7, emphasis added.

Our Savior has the ability to heal more than just the body. He has the power to heal those who are "afflicted in *any* manner". During His ministry among the Jews, our Savior testified that he had been commissioned by the Father to "heal the brokenhearted, to preach deliverance to the captives, and recovering of sight to the blind, to set at liberty them that are bruised".[4] Those who hurt us often break our hearts. We become bruised. And when we fail to forgive we become blind, captives of our own making. This simple poem once came to my mind:

> When I forgave my fellowman
> I set a prisoner free.
> And in the deed I came to know
> The prisoner was me.

An Incredible Thing Took Place

The divine help needed to forgive others comes most frequently through the Holy Ghost. The apostle Paul taught the Galatian Saints that "the fruit of the Spirit is love, joy, peace, longsuffering, gentleness, goodness, faith, meekness, temperance . . . ."[5]

In the book, *Tramp for the Lord*, Corrie ten Boom shares a powerful experience of forgiving others. Corrie and her sister Betsie had been imprisoned in a German concentration camp after being caught hiding Jews in their home in Nazi-occupied Holland. Betsie had died in the prison camp.

After the war Corrie traveled throughout Germany, testifying of God's message of repentance and forgiveness. One day after speaking in a church she recognized a man who had been one of the cruelest guards in the concentration camp. The man did not remember Corrie. But Corrie remembered him. The man had come forward to thank her for her message of God's forgiveness and to tell her he had become a Christian. Then the

---

[4] Luke 4:18

[5] Galatians 5:22

man held out his hand to shake Corrie's. But Corrie could not bring herself to shake his. She reached into her purse, pretending to look for something as an excuse not to shake his hand. So he held his hand out to her again:

> "Jesus, help me!" I prayed silently. "I can lift my hand. I can do that much. You supply the feeling."
>
> And so woodenly, mechanically, I thrust my hand into the one stretched out to me. And as I did, an incredible thing took place. The current started in my shoulder, raced down my arm, sprang into our joined hands. And then this healing warmth seemed to flood my whole being, bringing tears to my eyes.
>
> "I forgive you, brother!" I cried. "With all my heart."
>
> For a long moment we grasped each other's hands, the former guard and the former prisoner. I have never known God's love so intensely, as I did then. But even so, I realized it was not my love. I had tried, and did not have the power. It was the power of the Holy Spirit as recorded in Romans 5:5, ". . . because the love of God is shed abroad in our hearts by the Holy Ghost which is given unto us".[6]

The Savior Offers Help

Heavenly help and healing are available for those who exercise faith in the Lord's promises. And with that healing comes not only a powerful peace but a lifted burden. The Lord has promised:

> Come unto me, all ye that labour and are heavy laden, and I will give you rest.

---

[6] *Tramp for the Lord*, by Corrie ten Boom, 53-55.

Take my yoke upon you, and learn of me; for I am meek and lowly in heart: and ye shall find rest unto your souls.

For my yoke is easy, and my burden is light.[7]

---

[7] Matthew 11:28-30

7

Friends

*"If your so-called friends urge you to do anything you
know to be wrong, you be the one to make a stand for
the right, even if you stand alone."*
- President Thomas S. Monson[1]

From the age of 10 to the age of 15 I worked as a paperboy. At
the end of my route lived a boy named Eldon who became
one of my closest friends. Each day after delivering my papers I
would stop at his house to play, eat, play and then eat some
more. (I think Eldon's parents considered writing me off as a tax
deduction.)

On Sundays, I began delivering papers at 5 a.m. Around 6 a.m. I
would finish my route, ride to Eldon's house and tap on his
bedroom window. He would get up half-asleep and unlock the

---

[1] *Ensign*, May 2008

front door. We'd walk back to his bedroom. He'd crawl back in bed and I'd sleep on his floor for an hour or so. Then we'd get up, have a big bowl of cereal and I'd head back home.

At home, I would change into my Sunday clothes and then walk to church. Even though my parents did not attend, I rarely missed because I knew if I skipped church I would be sorely chastised by Eldon on Monday. He refused to let me be a slacker. He was a wonderful influence in my life. I never remember Eldon ever encouraging me to do something wrong.

Later the Lord blessed me with additional friends who continued to have a positive influence in my life. I credit my friends for getting me to the point where I received a strong testimony and could stand firm on my own.

Choosing Good Friends

But friends can also pull us in the opposite direction. President Gordon B. Hinckley (1910 - 2008), president of the Church of Jesus Christ of Latter-day Saints, has said, "Every boy or girl longs for friends. No one wishes to walk alone. The warmth, the comfort, the camaraderie of a friend mean everything to a boy or girl. That friend can be either an influence for good or an influence for evil."[2]

Even Joseph Smith sometimes chose friends that were not always the best influence on him. In fact, one of the reasons he was praying the night the angel Moroni appeared was to ask Heavenly Father to forgive him for poor choices he made in the company of certain friends. He wrote:

> During the space of time which intervened between the time I had the vision and the year eighteen hundred and twenty-three–having been forbidden to join any of the religious sects of the day, and being of very tender years, and persecuted by those who ought to have been my friends and to have treated me kindly, and if they supposed me to be deluded to have endeavored in a

---

[2] *Ensign*, November 2000

proper and affectionate manner to have reclaimed me—
I was left to all kinds of temptations; and, mingling with
all kinds of society, I frequently fell into many foolish
errors, and displayed the weakness of youth, and the
foibles of human nature; which, I am sorry to say, led
me into divers temptations, offensive in the sight of
God. In making this confession, no one need suppose
me guilty of any great or malignant sins. A disposition
to commit such was never in my nature. But I was guilty
of levity, and sometimes associated with jovial
company, etc., not consistent with that character which
ought to be maintained by one who was called of God
as I had been. But this will not seem very strange to any
one who recollects my youth, and is acquainted with my
native cheery temperament.

In consequence of these things, I often felt
condemned for my weakness and imperfections; when,
on the evening of the above-mentioned twenty-first of
September, after I had retired to my bed for the night, I
betook myself to prayer and supplication to Almighty
God for forgiveness of all my sins and follies, and also
for a manifestation to me, that I might know of my state
and standing before him; for I had full confidence in
obtaining a divine manifestation, as I previously had
one.[3]

Good friends lift you. They inspire you through word and deed
to be better than you are. They kindly correct when you need
to be nudged in a different direction. And they seek to live the
teachings of Jesus Christ.

So what should we do if we have friends that don't influence us
for the good? Jesus taught that sometimes we have to do the
difficult thing: "Therefore, if thy hand offend thee, cut it off; or
if thy brother offend thee and confess not and forsake not, he
shall be cut off. It is better for thee to enter into life maimed,

---

[3] Joseph Smith History 1:28-29

than having two hands, to go into hell."[4] In other words, it's better to be without friends than to be pulled down by them.

"I Don't Have Any Friends"

As a boy, my son Clint was somewhat quiet and shy. So making friends did not come easily for him. As he got older many of his close friends began to go down the wrong paths. Clint chose not to go with them. And though his standards helped him find new friends, it cost him the companionship of others. At times he was left at home with no one to "hang out" with but his parents. Not fun for a teenager!

During his senior year in high school I came home one Friday night to find him lying face down on the living room floor. I asked him what was wrong. He said, "Big snowmobiling party tonight, Dad. But of course, I'm not invited." He kept his face to the carpet because he didn't want me to see the tears.

I sat down and said, "Clint, sometimes it's lonely when you keep the commandments. Joseph Smith knew a great deal of loneliness. Jesus knew loneliness."

And then I said something I hoped would bring him some comfort. "And believe it or not, your example is influencing people. People are watching you."

That's when he got mad! I guess he'd heard that speech one too many times. He blurted out, "No one's watching, Dad! No one cares! Maybe they cared in your day, but no one cares anymore! So don't tell me people are watching me!"

I didn't know what else to say so I quietly walked away. Another lonely night for Clint.

Several months later, something significant happened. Clint had been asked to be one of the speakers at his seminary graduation. He did a great job. We were proud of him. After the

---

[4] JST Mark 9:40

program, a mother came up to me and asked, "Is Clint Carver your son?"

"Yes, he is," I said proudly.

"He did a nice job on his talk," she said.

"Thanks, I'll pass that along to him."

"Can I share something my son said about your son?"

"Sure. Who's your son?"

She pointed to a young man happily loading up on refreshments.

"Oh sure, I know your son. He was the star fullback of the state championship football team!"

She smiled. "That's right. When we came into the chapel tonight he saw your son sitting on the stand and said, 'You see that kid, Mom? That's Clint Carver. If he says something or does something it will always be the right thing.'"

Now let me interject something. Clint had deeply desired to be on one of the school athletic teams. He tried out several times for the basketball team but never made it. He had tried out for the golf team but never made it. At times he felt like a nobody in his school. But here was one of the school's top athletes telling his mother about this young man he had quietly been watching.

I waited until we got home and then shared with him what the mother had told me. Then I paused and said, "So nobody was watching, huh?"

The smile on his face and the moisture in his eyes told me how he felt – it had all been worth the price. There was a payoff for his faithfulness.

Had the loss of his friends been painful? Yes. Had he experienced loneliness? Yes. Had he followed the Lord's teachings anyway? Yes. That's faith! And his faith resulted in finding many new friends, including a wonderful girl whom he married for time and eternity. And three children who are now also watching.

8

Media

"And now I say unto you, all you that are desirous to follow the voice of the good shepherd, come ye out from the wicked, and be ye separate, and touch not their unclean things . . ."[1]

Do you have ants around your house? We occasionally have a colony or two appear in our yard. Most ants are fairly harmless but some species can sting or do serious damage to wood and surrounding structures.

Killing a colony of ants can be very difficult because the queen and most of the ants live deep in the ground where sprays can't reach them. However, researchers have found a very effective way to kill entire colonies. Foraging ants, the ones that hunt for food, eat the food they find and return to the colony. They feed

---

[1] Alma 5:57

the other ants through a process called trophallaxis – the exchange of regurgitated food. Specialists have developed something called *ant bait*. It is a food ants love mixed with a gentle poison. The foraging ants eat the bait but the poison does not immediately kill them. The poison works slowly enough that the foraging ants return to the colony, regurgitate the poisoned food and feed it to the other ants – including the queen! Thus wiping out the queen and her colony.

Poisoned Media

Today's media can be similar to ant bait. Most people enjoy watching television and movies. Years ago this kind of 'food' was wholesome and harmless. Though some of the modern media is blatantly evil, much of the media has been gently poisoned with "a few bad parts". The adversary is aware that if media is too offensive many people will not watch. So he adds just enough that people tolerate the bad parts and expose their minds and hearts to the gentle poison. Many share it with friends and family, mistakingly poisoning them also.

President Gordon B. Hinckley (1910 – 2008), the 15th president of the Church, has warned:

> There is so much of evil in this world. It seems to be everywhere—in television, in books, in magazines, in videos. Do not sit around watching videos of a sleazy nature. Do not do it. They will not help you. They will hurt you. You can become addicted to those things, and they will destroy you. I have seen it in the lives of many people.[2]

That's strong counsel from a prophet of God. But many do not sense the danger. One of my students was telling me about a movie he had seen. When I asked him if it was a wholesome movie he said, "It has a few bad parts, but it was hilarious." I winced a little and asked, "How many bad parts does a movie have to have before you won't watch it?" That made him stop

---

[2] *New Era*, January 2000

and think. That may be a question we should all ask ourselves. How much will we tolerate before we refuse to watch?

Contaminated Thoughts

The stomach has a way to deal with tainted food. It vomits it back out. The brain, however, is very different. Tainted images submitted to the brain are not easily removed. They can be long-lasting. One of my friends who served as a mission president told me that the elders in his mission who struggled most were those who had exposed their minds to pornographic images. They told him how difficult it was to keep the images from returning. President Russell M. Nelson, (1924 – current), 17th president of the Church, has confirmed that danger:

The body has means by which it can cleanse itself from the harmful effects of contaminated food or drink. But it cannot vomit back the poison of pornography. Once recorded, it always remains subject to recall, flashing its perverted images across your mind, with power to draw you away from the wholesome things in life. Avoid it like the plague![3]

"I Think He Is a Very Good Man"

In my years of teaching in the seminary and institute programs, I had the opportunity of associating with many outstanding teachers. Though not perfect, they have set an example for me in seeking to practice what we preach.

One such teacher is Mike Woodbury. One morning the school was having an assembly. Classes were excused for an hour. Instead of going to the assembly I decided to stay at my office and catch up on some lesson prep. Mike decided to go to the assembly.

An hour or so later one of my students stuck her head in my office to tell me that the assembly was over.

---

[3] *Ensign*, May 1999

"How was it?" I asked.

She paused and said something that caught me off guard: "Brother Woodbury is a very good man."

"Yes, he is," I said. "But what makes you say that?"

She explained that during the assembly one of the school's cheer teams performed a dance. She said that the outfits were not modest and some of the dance moves were suggestive.

Then she said, "I looked over at Brother Woodbury and he was looking at the floor. He never looked up during their performance. I think he is a very good man."

Losing the Help of the Spirit

Brother Woodbury was following the Lord's counsel to "let virtue garnish thy thoughts unceasingly".[4] The word *garnish* comes from a French word that originally meant to protect. The Lord has given a wonderful promise to those who protect their minds with virtuous thoughts:

> . . . then shall thy confidence wax strong in the presence of God; and the doctrine of the priesthood shall distil upon thy soul as the dews from heaven.
>
> The Holy Ghost shall be thy constant companion, and thy scepter an unchanging scepter of righteousness and truth; and thy dominion shall be an everlasting dominion, and without compulsory means it shall flow unto thee forever and ever.[5]

How important is it to have the Holy Spirit as a constant companion? President Gordon B. Hinckley has taught:

> There is no greater blessing that can come into our lives than the gift of the Holy Ghost—the companionship of the Holy Spirit to guide us, protect us, and bless us, to

---

[4] Doctrine and Covenants 121:45

[5] Ibid.

go, as it were, as a pillar before us and a flame to lead us in paths of righteousness and truth. That guiding power of the third member of the Godhead can be ours if we live worthy of it.[6]

On the other hand, the scriptures teach us of the high price we pay when we do not protect our thoughts: "And he that looketh upon a woman [or a man] to lust after her shall deny the faith, *and shall not have the Spirit*; and if he repents not he shall be cast out".[7]

What a great victory for Satan when our choice of media causes us to lose the companionship of a member of the Godhead!

A Priceless Gift

A friend of mine shared an experience that taught him how priceless the companionship of the Holy Ghost is. He had put his new baby in her crib and gone to the living room to read the newspaper. As he began reading he received a clear impression to check on the baby. He ignored the feeling because he had just barely put the baby to bed. The impression came twice more. Finally, he went to the baby's crib and found she had vomited and was choking to death. With tears in his eyes, he told me that the Holy Ghost had saved his baby's life. What if my friend had been reading or watching something offensive instead of reading the paper? Would he have been able to recognize the Spirit's prompting?

A Guideline for Media

I would often get a puzzled look from my students when I encouraged them to only watch media that is rated 'AF-13'.

They would often respond, "There's not an AF-13 rating, Brother Carver. Do you mean PG-13?"

---

[6] *Teachings of Gordon B. Hinckley,* 259

[7] Doctrine and Covenants 42:23, emphasis added

"Nope, I mean AF-13". They quickly understood what I meant when I began to quote: "If there is anything virtuous, lovely, or of good report or praiseworthy, we seek after these things."[8]

Counsel of the Lord's Servants

The First Presidency has counseled us:

> Do not attend, view, or participate in anything that is vulgar, immoral, violent, or pornographic in any way. Do not participate in anything that presents immorality or violence as acceptable. Have the courage to walk out of a movie, change your music, or turn off a computer, television, or mobile device if what you see or hear drives away the Spirit.[9]

Keeping our standards high can sometimes result in peer pressure from those around us. My daughter Christa once faced a situation that tested her faith in following the Lord's counsel regarding media.

"This Was My Big Chance"

"Starting junior high was a chance to meet new people and make new friends. I was filled with excitement and anticipation at the beginning of my 7th-grade year. I quickly made friends with a group of girls who were kind and welcoming. We sat by each other in classes, ate lunch together and passed notes in the hallways.

"On one particular Friday, they told me they were going to a party after school. They invited me to come. I was thrilled! My parents agreed as long as there would be parents at the party. They let me ride the bus home with one of the girls.

"Early into the evening we left her home for the party, talking and laughing all the way there. I walked inside and saw many

---

[8] Article of Faith 13

[9] *For the Strength of Youth*, Entertainment and Media

faces I recognized from school. Then my eyes rested on one person in particular. It was a boy I really liked. This would be the perfect opportunity to talk to him. And I would have several hours to work up the courage!

"We began playing a number of fun group games, but several people quickly became bored. One kid began scanning the movie collection and suggested a movie that I knew was not good. I watched in surprise as many nodded in agreement. The movie was removed from its cover and slid into the player. I panicked – I couldn't believe this was happening. This was my big chance to fit in with my new friends. I thought about staying and closing my eyes during the bad parts. No one would notice because the lights would be off. But they would notice if I left. And they would know why.

"I fought this battle silently in my heart as the lights turned off and people began claiming spots on the couches and floor. I stood up, walked from the living room to the kitchen and found the phone. When I returned and told my friends I was leaving, they were disappointed – but not nearly as much as I was. I envisioned the ride home with my father would be a lonesome one. This whole 'choosing the right' business was going to make for an awfully lonely year. Or so I thought.

"As I looked out the window at the night sky on the ride home, I don't know if I've ever felt more loved, or happier. My choice had been noticed by not only my friends but by my Heavenly Father. It was as if I were being embraced by Him; as if I could see in my mind His face smiling, expressing His joy in the decision I had made.

"And that decision, seemingly small and insignificant then, became a point of reference for decisions that have led to greater blessings and happiness than I ever thought possible."

Trading Up for Better Things

As we exercise faith in the Lord's standards there will be movies we won't watch, books we won't read and television shows we i. And there may possibly be friends we offend. But in exchange, there will be individuals whose hearts and hands are clean. There will be families that remain unspotted by the world. There will be marriages that stand steady and strong. And for all there will be a sweet peace that comes from the constant companionship of a member of the Godhead. These are blessings of faith in Jesus Christ.

9

Ministering

"Therefore they did watch over their people, and did nourish them with things pertaining to righteousness."[1]

Have you ever heard of a "bummer lamb"? The sheep industry uses this term to describe a lamb that has been separated from its mother or rejected by its mother at birth. A bummer lamb must be hand-fed and cared for until it is able to eat on its own.

President James E. Faust (1920 – 2007), a member of the Quorum of Twelve Apostles and First Presidency, shared an experience he had as a little boy when his father gave him a bummer lamb to care for.

---

[1] Mosiah 23:18

Responsibilities of Shepherds

"When I was a very small boy, my father found a lamb all alone out in the desert. The herd of sheep to which its mother belonged had moved on, and somehow the lamb got separated from its mother, and the shepherd must not have known that it was lost. Because it could not survive alone in the desert, my father picked it up and brought it home. To have left the lamb there would have meant certain death, either by falling prey to the coyotes or by starvation because it was so young that it still needed milk. Some sheep men call these lambs 'bummers'. My father gave the lamb to me and I became its shepherd.

"For several weeks I warmed cow's milk in a baby's bottle and fed the lamb. We became fast friends. I called him Nigh – why I don't remember. It began to grow. My lamb and I would play on the lawn. Sometimes we would lie together on the grass and I would lay my head on its soft, woolly side and look up at the blue sky and the white billowing clouds. I did not lock my lamb up during the day. It would not run away. It soon learned to eat grass. I could call my lamb from anywhere in the yard by just imitating as best I could the bleating sound of a sheep: Baa. Baa.

"One night there came a terrible storm. I forgot to put my lamb in the barn that night as I should have done. I went to bed. My little friend was frightened in the storm, and I could hear it bleating. I knew that I should help my pet, but I wanted to stay safe, warm, and dry in my bed. I didn't get up as I should have done. The next morning I went out to find my lamb dead. A dog had also heard its bleating cry and killed it. My heart was broken. I had not been a good shepherd or steward of that which my father had entrusted to me. My father said, 'Son, couldn't I trust you to take care of just one lamb?' My father's remark hurt me more than losing my woolly friend. I resolved that day, as a little boy, that I would try never again to neglect my stewardship as a shepherd if I were ever placed in that position again.

"Not too many years thereafter I was called as a junior companion to a home teacher. There were times when it was so cold or stormy and I wanted to stay home and be comfortable, but in my mind's ear I could hear my little lamb bleating, and I knew I needed to be a good shepherd and go with my senior companion."[2]

Shepherds in Israel

In our ward and stake callings and in our ministering assignments we are given the opportunity to serve as shepherds for the Lord's sheep. In these stewardships it is easy to develop a casual mindset and become less than faithful. Several years ago a friend shared with me an experience he had as a young home teacher. Each time I read his experience I am motivated to be more faithful in my calling to minister.

Three Lives Were Changed

"Shortly after becoming a newly-minted teacher in the Aaronic Priesthood, I was assigned to be the home teaching companion to a newly-returned missionary, the bishop's son, Tommy Tucker. He owned a cool Chevy hardtop with glass-pack mufflers. It was a 'cherry' automobile as we used to say. So I was happy for the assignment.

"Brother Tucker picked me up one evening and we went to the first house, an apartment. I had never seen these people at Church or anywhere else for that matter. And they were not only strangers, they were strange. The apartment smelled like coffee and the television was blaring. My returned missionary companion asked the man of the house, a small fellow who was nearly deaf, if he could turn the television down. His wife hollered into his ear to turn it down. He said he couldn't hear it then, and turned it up. The noise was deafening. We began talking with their son, about 20 years old, who had come into the room. My companion began asking him questions. Was he active in the Church? No. When was the last time he had attended? He couldn't remember. The questions embarrassed him and they embarrassed me. Did this returned missionary

---

[2] *Ensign*, May 1995.

have to be so blunt? One doesn't talk like this to perfect strangers. Not even to imperfect strangers.

"After offering a prayer in that deafening room my companion told this fellow we would pick him up for Church on Sunday morning. He protested that he had no Sunday clothes. Brother Tucker stated that we would come by anyway. We left. I was glad to be out of there.

"The next place was a basement apartment and the tenant an old man. We sat on an ancient couch, a coffee table between us and the man. On the coffee table was an open five-pound coffee can. It contained pipe tobacco, a very pungent blend. A collection of well-used pipes ringed the can, held in place by metal clips. After some initial chit-chat, my companion said bluntly, 'I see you have a Word of Wisdom problem.' I was mortified at this! I wanted to crawl under the table. I felt sorry that I had come. I felt sorry that I had been assigned to this insensitive owner of a very cool car. And I felt even sorrier for this old gentleman.

"'Yes,' he said, quietly, his head hanging. 'I guess I do.'

"They talked some more, then the same, 'We'll pick you up for church on Sunday,' directive was issued. The old man gave the same excuse – no clothes. My partner said we would come by anyway. "Wear whatever you have," he told the man. We prayed and then left. I was ready to ask for a new partner. But what could I do? He was the bishop's son.

"That Sunday, after Priesthood meeting, Brother Tucker and I drove to the first apartment. We parked the Chevy and knocked on the door. I was expecting, at best, an excuse. I was hoping for an excuse. This home teaching thing had turned out to be painful business. But the door opened and out stepped our friend dressed in a new suit and ready for Church. He looked fresh and clean and eager.

"The three of us drove to the old man's place. We walked down the stairs and knocked. He came out of the apartment, dressed and ready for Church. Suit and tie. Hair slicked back. He looked younger. It was unbelievable. The four of us drove to Church and sat together through Sunday School. Later that evening we returned to Sacrament meeting.

"The short story is that the young man soon after served a mission. And when he returned he married in the temple. And the old man, to my knowledge, never missed another meeting.

"The two home teaching visits had taken perhaps a total of one hour. And two lives were forever changed. Make that three. I learned the lesson that Alma taught his son Shiblon about being bold, but not overbearing. And I discovered the great joy of bringing souls to Christ. Some years later I was called to serve in southern Brazil. But I knew before I went, thanks in part to Tommy Tucker, what a ministering is really all about."[3]

Faithful Over a Few Things

Those who exercise faith in fulfilling their callings will someday receive the Lord's high praise and highest rewards: "His lord said unto him, Well done, thou good and faithful servant: thou hast been faithful over a few things, I will make thee ruler over many things: enter thou into the joy of thy lord."[4]

---

[3] Story by Rex Thomas Price (in the author's possession)

[4] Matthew 25:21

63

10

Missions

"And now, behold, I say unto you, that the thing which will be of the most worth unto you will be to declare repentance unto this people, that you may bring souls unto me, that you may rest with them in the kingdom of my Father."[1]

One of the last directives the Lord gave to the apostles prior to His ascension to heaven was to take the Gospel to all the world. Matthew, an apostle who was with the Lord on that occasion, wrote of that commission:

> Go ye therefore, and teach all nations, baptizing them in the name of the Father, and of the Son, and of the Holy Ghost: Teaching them to observe all things

---

[1] Doctrine and Covenants 15:6

whatsoever I have commanded you: and, lo, I am with you alway, even unto the end of the world. Amen.[2]

In the Lord's Day, the army of missionaries was very small. In our day that number has swelled to the hundreds of thousands. Faithful missionaries, young and old, male and female, are responding to a prophet's call to "seek out the righteous where'er they may be".[3] Setting aside schooling, jobs, friends, and family they go forth into all the world in search of those they can bring to Jesus Christ.

Isaiah prophesied of these Latter-day heroes: "Thus saith the Lord God: Behold, I will lift up mine hand to the Gentiles, and set up my standard to the people; and they shall bring thy sons in their arms, and thy daughters shall be carried upon their shoulders."[4]

Nephi explained the meaning of this passage:

> And it meaneth that the time cometh that after all the house of Israel have been scattered and confounded, that the Lord God will raise up a mighty nation among the Gentiles, yea, even upon the face of this land; and by them shall our seed be scattered.
>
> And after our seed is scattered the Lord God will proceed to do a marvelous work among the Gentiles, which shall be of great worth unto our seed; wherefore, it is likened unto their being nourished by the Gentiles and being carried in their arms and upon their shoulders.
>
> Wherefore, he will bring them again out of captivity, and they shall be gathered together to the lands of their inheritance; and they shall be brought out of obscurity and out of darkness; and they shall

---

[2] Matthew 28:19-20

[3] "Ye Elders of Israel", *Hymns*, 319

[4] Isaiah 49:22

know that the Lord is their Savior and their Redeemer, the Mighty One of Israel.[5]

Fishers and Hunters

Some of the Lord's missionaries serve in areas of the world where they are able to help bring many people to His Gospel. Others find themselves in places where those who join the Church are much fewer. It is as Jeremiah prophesied: "Behold, I will send for many fishers, saith the Lord, and they shall fish them; and after will I send for many hunters, and they shall hunt them from every mountain, and from every hill, and out of the holes of the rocks."[6]

Some missionaries are as fishers and gather nets filled with the faithful. Others find only a few as they hunt them down one by one.

The missionaries who see a smaller harvest may sometimes wonder, "Was the sacrifice of time and money worth the small harvest?" A story told by President James E. Faust, (1920 – 2007) a member of the Quorum of the Twelve Apostles and First Presidency, teaches the importance of bringing even one soul to the Savior.

One Dirty Little Irish Kid

"Those of us who have served missions have seen the miracle in the lives of some we have taught as they have come to realize that they are sons and daughters of God. Many years ago an elder who served a mission in the British Isles said at the end of his labors, 'I think my mission has been a failure. I have labored all my days as a missionary here and I have only baptized one dirty little Irish kid. That is all I baptized.'

---

[5] 1 Nephi 22:7-8, 12

[6] Jeremiah 16:16

"Years later, after his return to his home in Montana, he had a visitor come to his home who asked, 'Are you the elder who served a mission in the British Isles in 1873?'

"'Yes.'

"Then the man went on, 'And do you remember having said that you thought your mission was a failure because you had only baptized one dirty little Irish kid?'

"He said, 'Yes.'

"The visitor put out his hand and said, 'I would like to shake hands with you. My name is Charles A. Callis, of the Council of the Twelve of The Church of Jesus Christ of Latter-day Saints. I am that dirty little Irish kid that you baptized on your mission.'

"That little Irish boy came to a knowledge of his potential as a son of God. Elder Callis left a lasting legacy for his large family. Serving as a mission president for 25 years and in his apostolic ministry for 13 years, he blessed the lives of literally thousands. I feel privileged to have known this great Apostle of the Lord when I was a young man."[7]

The Parker Boy

A number of years ago Elder Boyd K. Packer (1924 – 2015), a member of the Quorum of the Twelve Apostles, shared an experience from the journals of the handcart pioneers. It has great application to those who go forth in missionary service.

"In the late 1850s, many converts from Europe were struggling to reach the Great Salt Lake Valley. Many were too poor to afford the open and the covered wagons and had to walk, pushing their meager belongings in handcarts. Some of the most touching and tragic moments in the history of the Church accompanied these handcart pioneers.

"One such company was commanded by a Brother McArthur. Archer Walters, an English convert who was with the company,

---

[7] *Ensign*, May 2001

recorded in his diary under July 2, 1856, this sentence: 'Brother Parker's little boy, age six, was lost, and the father went back to hunt him'.

"The boy, Arthur, was next youngest of four children of Robert and Ann Parker. Three days earlier the company had hurriedly made camp in the face of a sudden thunderstorm. It was then the boy was missed. The parents had thought him to be playing along the way with the other children.

"Someone remembered earlier in the day, when they had stopped, that they had seen the little boy settle down to rest under the shade of some brush.

"Now most of you have little children and you know how quickly a tired little six-year-old could fall asleep on a sultry summer day and how soundly he could sleep, so that even the noise of the camp moving on might not awaken him.

"For two days the company remained, and all of the men searched for him. Then on July 2, with no alternative, the company was ordered west.

"Robert Parker, as the diary records, went back alone to search once more for his little son. As he was leaving camp, his wife pinned a bright shawl about his shoulders with words such as these: 'If you find him dead, wrap him in the shawl to bury him. If you find him alive, you could use this as a flag to signal us.'

"She, with the other little children, took the handcart and struggled along with the company.

"Out on the trail each night Ann Parker kept watch. At sundown on July 5, as they were watching, they saw a figure approaching from the east! Then, in the rays of the setting sun, she saw the glimmer of the bright red shawl.

"One of the diaries records: 'Ann Parker fell in a pitiful heap upon the sand, and that night, for the first time in six nights, she slept.'

"Under July 5, Brother Walters recorded: 'Brother Parker came into camp with a little boy that had been lost. Great joy through the camp. The mother's joy I cannot describe.'

"We do not know all of the details. A nameless woodsman – I've often wondered how unlikely it was that a woodsman should be there – found the little boy and described him as being sick with illness and with terror, and he cared for him until his father found him.

"So here a story, commonplace in its day, ends – except for a question. How would you, in Ann Parker's place, feel toward the nameless woodsman had he saved your little son? Would there be any end to your gratitude?

"To sense this is to feel something of the gratitude our Father must feel toward any of us who saves one of his children."[8]

Nothing Else Compares

President Russell M. Nelson has taught that:

> These surely are the latter days, and the Lord is hastening His work to gather Israel. That gathering is the most important thing taking place on earth today. Nothing else compares in magnitude, nothing else compares in importance, nothing else compares in majesty. And if you choose to, if you want to, you can be a big part of it. You can be a big part of something big, something grand, something majestic![9]

The Lord's Promise to the Gatherers

The Lord invites His servants to venture forth and rescue those who are suffering, stranded or seeking. Whether they bring few or many into His kingdom, those who are faithful in fulfilling the Lord's invitation will come to realize His promise: "And if it so be that you should labor all your days in crying repentance unto

---

[8] *Ensign*, November 1974

[9] "Hope of Israel" (worldwide youth devotional, June 3, 2018)

this people, and bring, save it be one soul unto me, how great shall be your joy with him in the kingdom of my Father!"[10]

---

[10] Doctrine and Covenants 18:15

11

Modesty

"In the gospel of Jesus Christ, modesty in appearance is always in fashion. Our standards are not socially negotiable."
- Elder Jeffrey R. Holland[1]

As a young boy I always looked forward to our family trips to American Falls, Idaho. Fishing at the local dam was some of the best I've ever experienced. The trout were big and put up a wonderful fight when you hooked into one of them. The critical part was the bait. There was little chance of catching the trout if you weren't using the right bait.

When the trout weren't biting we sometimes went to a different part of the dam to fish for what we called *chubb*. You could use almost any kind of bait to catch chubb. But they weren't fun to

---

[1] *Ensign*, November 2005

catch. They put up almost no fight. It was like pulling in a soggy tennis shoe. And they weren't the kind of fish anyone ate. If you caught chubb you were encouraged to kill them because they ate trout eggs. We usually caught one or two and then looked for something else to do.

Have you ever considered that people use *bait* to *catch* people? There are many different kinds of *baits* that you can use in your dating years. One of those is the way you dress. Modesty and immodesty are both powerful baits. But they attract very different kinds of *fish*. Immodesty can bring a significant amount of interest, but it will never attract worthy priesthood holders or virtuous young women.

What Young Men Can Do

Elder Richard G. Scott (1928 – 2015), a member of the Quorum of the Twelve Apostles, gave some excellent suggestions on what young men can do to help promote modesty:

> So many of our own young women sacrifice their God-given endowment of femininity, deep spirituality, and a caring interest in others on the altar of popular, worldly opinion. Young men, let such young women know that you will not seek an eternal companion from those that are overcome by worldly trends. Many dress and act immodestly because they are told that is what you want. In sensitive ways, communicate how distasteful revealing attire is to you, a worthy young man, and how it stimulates unwanted emotions from what you see against your will.
>
> Those young women who do embrace conservative dress standards and exhibit the attributes of a devoted Latter-day Saint are often criticized for not being 'with it.' Encourage them by expressing gratitude for their worthy example. Thank them for doing what is pleasing to the Lord and in time will bless their own husband and children. Many young women have returned to

righteousness because of the example and understanding support of a worthy priesthood bearer. Perhaps a group of you could frankly discuss your concern in an appropriate setting such as a Sunday School or seminary class. Will you begin a private crusade to help young women understand how precious they are to God and attractive to you as they magnify their feminine traits and divinely given attributes of womanhood? You might even help mold the character and devotion of your own future eternal companion.

As a brother, you can have a powerful, positive influence in your sister's life. Compliment her when she looks especially nice. She may listen to you more than to your parents when you suggest that she wear modest clothing. Simple courtesies like opening the door for her and building her self-esteem will encourage her to find her real worth.[2]

Modest Are the Hottest

In 2003 two Latter-day Saint young men from Gilbert, Arizona followed such counsel. They decided to communicate to the girls in their high school their feelings about modesty. Andrew Packer and Arthur Schmeiser, then 15 and 18 years old, had T-shirts printed with "*Modest are the hottest!*" on the front. On the back "*I love modest women*" was printed in nine different languages. Arthur said, "It's hard to keep our thoughts clean when girls are wearing practically nothing. We wanted to show that we're passionate about this. We really do like girls who dress modestly."

But Arthur and Andrew weren't the only males in their school who wanted to make a statement about modesty. Classmates soon began requesting the T-shirts. Eventually, the two young

---

[2] *Ensign*, May 2000

men had nearly 200 professionally-printed shirts purchased and worn by young men at their high school.

Did it make a difference? Arthur said, "We've had a lot of girls thank us for wearing the shirts." Andrew added, "They tell us they feel like they can dress more modestly now without being made fun of. It's cool to take a stand."[3]

Petitioning for Modest Clothing

Finding clothing that is both modest and attractive is not an easy task for a young woman. Fashions for women have become increasingly immodest. A group of young Latter-day Saint girls in the Red Bridge Ward of the Olathe Kansas Stake decided to do something about it.

The idea for the project began in December of 2000 when Young Women President Cynthia Cockriel and her daughter Amanda were shopping for modest clothing. Frustrated with the limited availability, Sister Cockriel expressed her concerns to the manager of a popular retail store. The manager not only listened but asked Sister Cockriel and the young women of her ward to present ideas and descriptions of fashions they would like to see in the store.

Sister Cockriel and the young women spent four months preparing. They then presented a fashion show in which the branch divisional manager, store manager, and department manager attended. Seventeen young women modeled modest clothing and displayed picture boards of modest dresses they had found. Liz Christensen, the Laurel president, explained to the managers: "There is a strong customer base you currently miss at your store. It may not be a majority, but we hope to have shown you that it is big enough to make a difference in your business." The managers listened and began increasing the number of modest dresses on the racks. Different stores within the chain also expressed interest.

---

[3] *Church News*, Saturday, March 8, 2003

The *Kansas City Star* carried the initial story of these young women but the news quickly spread. The story was featured in *The Wall Street Journal* and several girls were interviewed by the *British Broadcasting Corporation*. Youth and parents from as far away as England and China began contacting the young women to express gratitude.

The impact of that small group of girls continues to grow. Young women and women throughout the country have joined in petitioning national chains and designers for more modest clothing.[4]

"No Crown Is Worth That"

The modesty Katie Millar demonstrated in winning Miss Utah 2006 started long before she entered the pageant. Katie was raised in a Latter-day Saint home where modesty was taught and practiced. That modesty was apparent in what Katie wore to school, at school dances, and in competitions. She and her mother teamed together to sew modest prom dresses and costumes.

Being Miss Utah gave Katie the opportunity to compete for Miss America. And while many appreciate the concept of modesty, it is certainly not promoted in the national competition.

When Katie began to select clothing for the pageant she was plainly told that her modesty would cost her the chance for victory. Designers strongly encouraged her to choose differently. But Katie was determined to prove that a person can and should be modest even on a national stage.

Katie made it as one of the top 10 finalists. In the final competition, contestants were asked to select and wear an evening gown and a swimsuit. Not only was her gown modest, but Katie was the only one to walk onstage in a one-piece swimsuit.

---

[4] *New Era*, January 2002

After the competition, Katie was surprised when a fellow Utahn approached her and chastised her for her modesty. "You were our one chance for Miss America and you blew it," he told Katie.

"I'm sorry, sir," she replied, "I can't change who I am. I guess no crown is worth it."[5]

A Greater Win

Katie didn't win Miss America. But she won the respect of thousands who were touched by the example of a young woman who refused to compromise her modesty. In the glare of a national spotlight Katie never wilted. She let her own light shine as someone who was more concerned with faith than with fashion.

---

[5] *Church News*, Saturday, January 26, 2008

12

Patriarchal Blessings

*"A patriarchal blessing contains chapters from your
life's book of possibilities. To you it will be as a
lighthouse on a hill, warning of dangers, and directing
you to the tranquility of safe harbors."*
– President Thomas S. Monson[1]

I grew up in a home with wonderful parents but neither was active in the church. So I learned about patriarchal blessings through my friends. After hearing that a patriarchal blessing could provide encouragement and direction to my life I eagerly met with my bishop to obtain a recommend.

I remember very clearly the day I got my blessing. I was seventeen years old and planning on serving a mission. My mother came with me to support me but told me that she had

---

[1] *Ensign*, May 1999

very little faith in the concept of patriarchal blessings. (She later became deeply converted to the Gospel and served many years as a temple worker.)

Our patriarch was Karl Storey. I had never met him. He knew nothing of me. I was to learn that day that patriarchal blessings do not come from patriarchs. They come from God.

In my blessing the patriarch said things he could not have known about me. He stated that I would serve in a foreign country and that I would be able to express myself in a foreign language. He didn't know that I had been impressed at the age of thirteen that I would serve a mission to Germany. Nor was he aware that I had already taken five years of German classes in junior high and high school.

He mentioned other details in my blessing that surprised even my mother. She asked me afterward, "Did you talk with the patriarch and tell him anything of those things he mentioned in the blessing?" I told her I hadn't discussed anything with him.

Several years later, while preparing to serve a mission, I realized there were several things in my patriarchal blessing that I knew would never be fulfilled. The blessing stated:

1. My parents would support me on my mission.

2. They would be blessed for supporting me.

3. They would be proud of me.

My parents were not happy about my plans to serve a mission call. Though I had saved a considerable amount of money for my mission I knew it wouldn't be enough. My father told me that he would pay for what I couldn't but that I would pay back "every penny" when I got home. So I already knew they wouldn't support me financially. And I knew they wouldn't be proud of me. I just dismissed those three promises as something patriarchs probably say to everyone.

But those promises had come from my Father in heaven. Not the patriarch. And I would watch all three promises come to pass.

I was called to serve in the German Central Mission. About a year into my mission my savings ran out. I wrote to my dad and asked him to please start sending money. I reassured him I would pay it all back when I got home. He and my mother sent the money every month.

Somewhere near the end of my mission my father sent me a letter that deeply surprised me. He said that I didn't need to repay the money when I got home. Promise one fulfilled. I learned that my mother had gotten a very good job and it was adding significant income to our family. Promise two fulfilled.

Shortly after returning home I was approached by one of my dad's friends who was active in the Church. He worked with my father and knew of my dad's resentment of my going on a mission. He told me he had been speaking with my father and had asked him how he felt now that I was back home.

"Do you know what your father said?" he asked. "Your father said, 'I'm pretty proud of my son.'"

Despite my disbelief, all three promises were fulfilled in exactness.

Unfulfilled Promises

A patriarchal blessing is sometimes referred to as the "If Blessing". The promises will be fulfilled *if* we are faithful.

But there are times when patriarchal blessings seem unfulfilled even when a person has demonstrated personal worthiness and obedience. President Boyd K. Packer, member of the Quorum of the Twelve Apostles and president of the Quorum, stated:

> Sometimes someone will worry because a promise made in a patriarchal blessing is not yet fulfilled. For instance, a blessing may indicate that a member will be married, and they do not find a companion. That does not mean that the blessing will go unfulfilled. It is well to know that things happen in the Lord's due time, not always in ours. Things of an eternal nature have no boundaries. From the premortal existence to our

existence beyond the veils of death, our life is an eternal life.[2]

Many Beautiful Daughters

And there are times when the meaning of a promised blessing can be misunderstood. President James E. Faust, a former member of the First Presidency, shared a promise from his father's patriarchal blessing stating his father would be blessed with "many beautiful daughters". His father and mother were blessed with five sons, no daughters. President Faust then shared this insight:

> This last summer when we had a family reunion, I saw my father's granddaughters moving about tending to the food and ministering to the young children and the elderly, and the realization came to me that Father's blessing had been literally fulfilled; he has, indeed, many beautiful daughters. The patriarch who gave my father his blessing had spiritual vision to see beyond this life. There was a disappearance of the dividing line between time and eternity.[3]

A friend of mine shared an experience regarding a promise in his patriarchal blessing that seemed impossible to be fulfilled.

That Promise Will Never Come True

"One Sabbath morning our Sunday School teacher taught my teenage class a lesson about how a patriarchal blessing can be a guide in our lives. She encouraged us to visit the patriarch and receive our blessing. Her words made a deep impression on me.

"At the conclusion of Sunday School, without telling my parents or asking permission, I walked a half-mile to the patriarch's home and knocked on his door. He invited me in and seated me at the end of a long dining room table. His wife sat with a ledger

---

[2] *Ensign*, Nov. 2002

[3] *Ensign*, November 1996

book at the other end of the table. Standing behind me with his hands on my head the patriarch began the blessing. He identified my lineage and then promised, 'As you will be true and faithful . . . great blessings are in store for you.' He would pause at the end of each phrase as his wife wrote his words in the ledger.

"He continued, 'If you will make use of the talents with which the Lord has blessed you, it will be your privilege to fill a mission for the Church of Jesus Christ and your voice shall be heard in song and the spoken word among the nations of the earth.'

"Those words, 'among the nations of the earth' entered my mind years later as I prepared to open my mission call. Expecting to be called to a foreign land, I was deeply surprised to be called to serve in the Central States Mission with headquarters in Independence, Missouri.

"'Well,' I thought, 'that patriarchal promise will never come true.'

"Many years later I became a second tenor in the Tabernacle Choir. And it would be several more years of listening to Elder Richard L. Evans introduce choir broadcasts as "Music and the Spoken Word" before I realized they were almost the same words spoken in my patriarchal blessing.

"It was my privilege to serve more than 20 years in the choir. Through broadcasts, recordings and tours to fourteen countries my voice truly was 'heard in song and the spoken word among the nations of the earth'".[4]

A Personal Liahona

President Thomas S. Monson (1927 – 2018), sixteenth president of the Church, has stated that a patriarchal blessing can be a personal Liahona to guide us:

> Your patriarchal blessing is yours and yours alone. It may be brief or lengthy, simple or profound. Length and

---

[4] Story in the author's possession

language do not a patriarchal blessing make. It is the Spirit that conveys the true meaning. Your blessing is not to be folded neatly and tucked away. It is not to be framed or published. Rather, it is to be read. It is to be loved. It is to be followed. Your patriarchal blessing will see you through the darkest night. It will guide you through life's dangers. Unlike the struggling bomber of yesteryear, lost in the desert wastes, the sands and storms of life will not destroy you on your eternal flight. Your patriarchal blessing is to you a personal Liahona to chart your course and guide your way.[5]

And, like the Liahona, it requires our obedience, our patience . . . and our faith!

---

[5] *Ensign*, November 1986

13

Prayer

*"I have had prayers answered. Those answers were
most clear when what I wanted was silenced by an
overpowering need to know what God wanted. It is then
that the answer from a loving Heavenly Father can be
spoken to the mind by the still, small voice and can be
written on the heart."*
– President Henry B. Eyring[1]

I once began a seminary lesson by saying something that
totally surprised my students. I had a large black marker in
my hand and said, "Last night I found a verse in the Book of
Mormon that is completely false. I'd like you to turn to Mormon
9:21 with me and let's blot it out with this marker."

---

[1] *Ensign*, November 2000

My students looked at me suspiciously. They sensed I was teasing, but they were curious. So they turned and read Mormon 9:21: "Behold, I say unto you that whoso believeth in Christ, doubting nothing, whatsoever he shall ask the Father in the name of Christ it shall be granted him; and this promise is unto all, even unto the ends of the earth."

I then asked, "How many of you have ever asked for something in prayer that you didn't get?"

Quite a few hands went up.

"So this verse can't possibly be true. It says whatsoever we ask for will be granted. We've all asked for things we didn't get. So I think it's best to strike out this verse so we're not disappointed anymore."

My students smiled skeptically. I continued.

"Let me prove my point. When I was about six years old my two favorite television shows were *Superman* and *Mighty Mouse*. I loved these shows because both superheroes could do something I desperately wanted to do – fly!

"One summer morning I woke up with a great idea. I'd been told in Primary that Heavenly Father hears our prayers and will answer them if we ask in faith. I knelt at my bedside and told Heavenly Father how desperately I wanted to fly. I told Him I knew I could do it if He helped me. Convinced that my prayer would be answered, I walked into our kitchen where my mother was preparing breakfast. She asked if I was ready for some pancakes. I looked at her as if to say, 'Mom, breakfast is kid's stuff. I've got a lot more exciting things to do.'

"I walked into the bathroom, pinned a towel around my neck (everyone knows you can't fly without a cape) and then stuffed a washcloth under my shirt so it looked like I had muscles like Mighty Mouse and Superman. I walked out the front door and onto our porch. The porch was about three feet high. I remember saying one more prayer just to make sure: 'Please, please, please Heavenly Father, please help me fly.'

"I opened my eyes, took a deep breath and jumped. Suddenly I was flying around the neighborhood and up into the clouds."

My students were now looking at me *very* skeptically.

"Is that what happened?" I asked.

"No, you landed in a big pile on the ground," one of my students joked.

"Exactly. I didn't fly. Even though I did everything in Mormon 9:21. So you see why it's important that we scratch out that verse?"

My students weren't sure how to respond. No one said anything. Then I told them that one day I read something in the Bible Dictionary that totally changed my understanding of that verse. And it totally changed my understanding of prayer.

> Prayer is the act by which the will of the Father and the will of the child are brought into correspondence with each other. The object of prayer is not to change the will of God, but to secure for ourselves and for others blessings that God is already willing to grant, but that are made conditional on our asking for them.
>
> Christians are taught to pray in Christ's name. We pray in Christ's name when our mind is the mind of Christ, and our wishes the wishes of Christ . . . Many prayers remain unanswered because they are not in Christ's name at all; they in no way represent his mind, but spring out of the selfishness of man's heart.[2]

I told my students that I finally understood why many of my prayers had not been answered. Even though I was closing my prayer "in the name of Jesus Christ", my prayers weren't really in His name because I wasn't asking for what He would have asked.

---

[2] Bible Dictionary, Topic: *Prayer*, pp. 752-53

I invited them to read another scripture with me: "Whatsoever you ask the Father in my name it shall be given unto you, that is expedient for you."[3]

I explained that the word *expedient* means *needful or necessary*. And the Lord has taught us how to know if something is expedient:

> Ask the Father in my name, in faith believing that you shall receive, and you shall have the Holy Ghost, which manifesteth all things which are expedient unto the children of men.[4]

In other words, if we listen to the promptings of the Spirit we will know what we should ask for, thus making our prayers truly in the name of Jesus Christ.

Brailee Ombach Saunders learned this powerful principle when her mother was diagnosed with cancer. You can imagine what Brailee prayed for.

"I Had to Learn to Ask for the Right Things "

"It's funny how it all works out. Someone gets sick and your prayers are extra sincere for that person to get better. My mother's diagnosis of cancer in March of 2001 was no exception. She was only thirty-four. I was eleven and my two brothers were eight and five. Even worse, it was an unknown cancer. With an unknown cause and an unknown cure, we were all facing a serious test of our faith.

"Priesthood blessing upon blessing, prayer upon prayer, treatment upon treatment, nothing seemed to work. My prayers, along with countless others, went unanswered. I was at the end of my rope. How could God just take her from me? What did I do wrong? Did I really deserve this? Hate, anger, and

---

[3] Doctrine and Covenants 88:64

[4] Doctrine and Covenants 18:18

frustration filled my life for several weeks. I even stopped praying.

"Then on September 11, 2001, my parent's 14th wedding anniversary, things got a lot worse. My mom awoke to a paralyzed body and without the ability to speak. She had suffered a stroke during the night.

"As I look back now there were many mighty miracles in the coming weeks. But at the time I felt only heartache and despair. Slowly though, I began to realize it was time to say goodbye. Don't get me wrong, I didn't transform overnight. I held onto my pride and kept praying for her to be healed. But on October 8, 2001, my morning prayer went something like this: 'I know it is time for her to go, Heavenly Father. I have been selfish. All I ask is three things before you take her. Please, will you have my dad there holding her hand? Please have a good friend there to visit and cheer her up. And please have someone there to support my dad in this time of need. Please, God?'

"I went to school that morning. Everything went as usual until the intercom called my name to come down to the office. Immediately I knew why. I didn't realize God would have jumped into action so fast. My grandparents greeted my brothers and me at the office. The two-minute car ride home seemed more like an hour.

"Upon arrival at our house, my dad greeted us at the front door with tears in the corners of his eyes. I asked him a simple question, 'Who was there?'

"His answered astonished me, even though it shouldn't have. 'I was there, holding your mom's hand. Sandy (my mom's best friend) had just left after a nice visit. And your grandparents were there making lunch for me.'

"The Spirit overwhelmed my heart and entire body with a deep love from my Father and Brother in Heaven. It took all my strength not to break down right there.

"I pondered that experience over the next few weeks and realized a simple truth. God does hear and answer our sincere prayers. But we have to ask for the right things. Then we need to put ourselves in God's hands and submit to His will and wisdom. His love is pure and whole. And I know He will never give us anything we cannot bear. He waited for me to be ready before He welcomed my mom back."[5]

Asking In His Name

When we learn to ask for what our Savior wants for us we are truly praying in His name. Brailee changed her petition to match with what the Lord wanted for her mother. No easy task. But a marvelous expression of faith in Jesus Christ.

---

[5] Story in the author's possession

14

Priesthood

"Miracles are everywhere to be found when priesthood callings are magnified. When faith replaces doubt, when selfless service eliminates selfish striving, the power of God brings to pass His purpose."
- President Thomas S. Monson[1]

My father loved tools. He had a workshop filled with them. When Father's Day, his birthday or Christmas came around he would say to us, "If you're wondering what to get me, just give me tools and I'll be happy." And he always was.

My father wanted to share his skill and love of tools with his five sons. When we reached the age of about twelve my dad began giving us tools as gifts. The first tools we received were hand tools: a wrench, a screwdriver, a hammer. Then Dad would

---

[1] *Ensign*, November 1999

watch to see if we took care of our tools. If we did, we received more at Christmas or on our next birthday.

As we got older and became more mature my dad began giving us power tools: a sander, a drill, a circular saw. He not only taught us how to use these tools but the importance of taking care of them. If he ever found us misusing the tools or not returning them to the proper place, we lost our privileges to his workshop for a while.

Our Father's Tools

Our Heavenly Father has tools, too. Two of His tools are the Aaronic and Melchizedek priesthoods. He allows these tools to be given to His worthy sons in order to bless the lives of all of His children.

The Aaronic Priesthood might be compared to hand tools. Beginning at the age of eleven, worthy young men become deacons and are given the authority to pass the Lord's sacrament. If a young man is faithful in this priesthood office he receives more *tools*. At the age of 14, a worthy young man can be ordained to the office of a teacher. A teacher has the responsibility to prepare the sacrament and to "watch over the church always, and be with and strengthen them".[2] When he turns 16, a worthy young man receives the *tools* to bless the sacrament and to baptize in the name of Jesus Christ.[3]

Those who magnify their Aaronic Priesthood will receive greater power and authority – even the *tools* of the Melchizedek priesthood. Imagine having the authority to give someone the gift of the Holy Ghost. Or to be able to call down the powers of heaven upon the head of someone who is sick. Neither kings nor presidents have the authority from God to do these things.

---

[2] D&C 20:53

[3] Doctrine and Covenants 20:46-60

These privileges are reserved for those who have been worthily ordained by one holding that priesthood.[4]

And even though the authority of the priesthood is bestowed only on worthy male members of the Church, the blessings of the priesthood are available to everyone. All of God's children, male and female, young and old, have the privilege of receiving the same saving ordinances administered by the priesthood.

All That My Father Hath

Are there additional *tools* our Father will share with the faithful? Carefully read this promise given to obedient priesthood holders:

> For whoso is faithful unto the obtaining these two priesthoods of which I have spoken, and the magnifying of their calling, are sanctified by the Spirit unto the renewing of their bodies.
>
> They become the sons of Moses and of Aaron and the seed of Abraham, and the church and kingdom, and the elect of God.
>
> And also all they who receive this priesthood receive me, saith the Lord;
>
> For he that receiveth my servants receiveth me;
>
> And he that receiveth me receiveth my Father;
>
> And he that receiveth my Father receiveth my Father's kingdom; therefore all that my Father hath shall be given unto him.[5]

All that the Father has! His power, His knowledge, His happiness, His glory! These are amazing promises to those who are faithful and magnify their callings.

---

[4] Doctrine and Covenants 20:38-43

[5] Doctrine and Covenants 84:33-38

Swapping Power for Pottage

The story of Esau has great significance for priesthood holders. Being the firstborn, Esau had the right to the birthright. After his father's death, he would have been given the leadership of the family. He would have received a double portion of his father's inheritance so he could care for his immediate family as well as his mother. But the scriptures say that Esau "despised his birthright".[6] This was clearly demonstrated on the occasion when Esau came home hungry and offered his birthright to Jacob in exchange for a mess of pottage. The word *mess* means *a serving*. And pottage is a kind of soup or stew. So Esau was willing to trade his birthright for a serving of soup!

In our day, Satan tries to convince priesthood holders to trade their priesthood power for a *mess of pottage*. Pornography, immorality, swearing and breaking the Word of Wisdom are poor exchanges for the powers of heaven. Those who remain faithful will experience many occasions when they will be grateful they didn't make that trade. Here's an experience from my own life.

He Slept Through the Night

In preparation for his mission, my son Clint needed four wisdom teeth pulled. The surgery didn't look like it would be a problem. So on the day of the procedure I was surprised to come home and find my son sitting on the edge of the sofa in great pain. My wife told me the surgery had gone well but the pain medication had made him nauseated. He had vomited it back up. Now he was not only sick to his stomach but in terrible pain. He couldn't even lie back on the couch because it made him dizzy and more nauseated.

We tried everything we could think of to bring him some relief: ice chips, medicine to settle his stomach, television to distract him. Nothing helped.

---

[6] Genesis 25:34

Around 9 o'clock that night I realized I needed to give Clint a blessing. He quickly agreed. I laid my hands upon his head and by the authority of the Melchizedek priesthood called upon the powers of heaven.

After the blessing, I told Clint I was going to go downstairs to say my prayers and that I would be back to check on him. I came back about ten minutes later and found him lying on the sofa, fast asleep. He slept through the entire night.

I later heard Clint bear his testimony concerning that experience. He testified that he knew the priesthood is real because nothing else could have brought him that kind of relief. Everything else had failed. I was not only thankful for the authority of the priesthood but deeply grateful I had kept my life clean in order to be able to access it.

Faith Unto Power

As worthy priesthood holders exercise faith unto righteousness they will be granted the authority to call upon the powers of heaven. And in accordance with our Father's will and wisdom, they will be given the power to bless His sons and daughters. To them, the Lord has given not only the tools but an incredible promise: "He that believeth on me, the works that I do shall he do also; and greater works than these shall he do."[7]

---

[7] John 14:12

15

Repentance

*"Therefore may God grant unto you, my brethren, that
ye may begin to exercise your faith unto repentance,
that ye begin to call upon his holy name, that he would
have mercy upon you..."*[1]

One of the heavy responsibilities a bishop carries is that of helping those who have been involved in serious sins. It is a huge exercise of faith for them to meet with the bishop and confess those transgressions. And they do so with the deep hope of being forgiven and becoming clean again.

I'm grateful that I don't remember many confessions during the time I served as bishop. My hope was to emulate the Savior and "remember them no more"[2]. But I do clearly remember a

---

[1] Alma 34:17

[2] Doctrine and Covenants 58:42

question asked by a person who had come to confess a serious sin. It is a question I believe all of us have in our hearts even though our sins may not be as serious. The question was this: "After all I've done, is there any hope of making it to the celestial kingdom?" And then the person quickly added, "Don't tell me it's possible just to make me feel good. I need you to be honest with me. I don't want to hope for the celestial kingdom if it really isn't possible anymore." Questions like these offer wonderful opportunities to help repentant persons understand not only the deep cleansing power of the atonement of Jesus Christ but the willingness of both the Father and the Son to forgive those who truly repent.

I invited this person to open the scriptures to Luke 15 where we read the Parable of the Prodigal Son. I pointed out that this young man had taken his inheritance and "wasted his substance with riotous living"[3]. Those six words give an ample description of the serious and repeated sins this son must have committed.

After finishing the parable I asked a number of questions:

- "It sounds like the son was gone for quite some time. How did the father know his son was coming home?" (He had been anxiously watching for him.)

- "What did the father do when he saw his son in the distance? (He *ran* to meet him, hugged and kissed him.)

- "Was the son repentant? Did he confess his sins?" (Yes.)

- "Did the son believe his father would forgive him?" (Probably not. He said he was no longer worthy to be called his son.)

---

[3] Luke 15:13

- "What did the father give his son?"

    o   The best robe: Only the finest. Nothing was held back.

    o   A ring: Reestablishing his family status and authority.

    o   Shoes for his feet: Restoring him from deep poverty.

    o   The fatted calf: A celebration of his son's return.

- "Did the father withhold anything because of his son's previous lifestyle?" (No.)

- "Who does the son represent?" (All of us – we are all sinners.)

- "Who does the father represent?" (Heavenly Father)

- "How does your Heavenly Father feel about your repentance?" (Great joy!)

- "Is He willing to forgive you?" (Eager to forgive!)

- "What blessings does He hold back from His repentant children?" (Nothing!)

Complete Forgiveness

The scriptures emphasize that the Lord is not only "mighty to save"[4] but that He is *willing to save*: "Come now, and let us reason together, saith the LORD: though your sins be as scarlet, they shall be as white as snow; though they be red like crimson, they shall be as wool."[5]

Elder Boyd K. Packer, a member of the Quorum of the Twelve Apostles, stated:

---

[4] 2 Nephi 31:19

[5] Isaiah 1:18

I repeat, save for the exception of the very few who defect to perdition, there is no habit, no addiction, no rebellion, no transgression, no apostasy, no crime exempted from the promise of complete forgiveness. That is the promise of the atonement of Christ.[6]

Nothing Held Back

I once heard a fireside speaker share a marvelous scriptural example of complete forgiveness. He pointed out that Alma the Younger and the sons of Mosiah were described as "the very vilest of sinners"[7]. Then he reminded us that after life-changing repentance Alma became the Lord's prophet and the sons of Mosiah became some of the most powerful missionaries that have ever lived. Their repentance was sincere. Their sins were completely washed away. They became "new creatures in Christ".[8] Neither rewards nor blessings were held back as a result of the lives they had once lived.

Weeping for the Wicked

In 1741 Jonathan Edwards, an American revivalist preacher, gave a sermon entitled, "Sinners in the Hand of an Angry God". In it Edwards stated:

> The God that holds you over the pit of hell, much as one holds a spider, or some loathsome insect over the fire, abhors you, and is dreadfully provoked: his wrath towards you burns like fire; he looks upon you as worthy of nothing else, but to be cast into the fire; he is of purer eyes than to bear to have you in his sight; you

---

[6] *Ensign*, November 1995

[7] Mosiah 28:4

[8] Mosiah 27:26

are ten thousand times more abominable in his eyes than the most hateful venomous serpent is in ours.[9]

Compare those words to what Enoch learned about God's feelings toward the sinner. Enoch was taken into the presence of God and shown the wickedness of the inhabitants of the earth. He then saw and bore record that the God of heaven began weeping for the wicked. In confusion, he asked, "How is it that the heavens weep, and shed forth their tears as the rains upon the mountains?"[10] Enoch seems to be asking, "Why is God weeping for the wicked?"

The Lord answered Enoch's question: "Satan shall be their father, and misery shall be their doom; and the whole heavens shall weep over them, even all the workmanship of mine hands; wherefore should not the heavens weep, seeing these shall suffer?"[11] The God of heaven is not a vindictive God. Neither He nor His Son takes joy in the sorrow and suffering of those who will not repent.

At the Heart of the Atonement of Jesus Christ

What lies at the heart of the Savior's atonement? What is found at the very center of the Father's gift of His Son to the world? The very core motivation of the Father's work is explained in one verse in the Gospel of St. John: "For God so loved the world, that he gave his only begotten Son, that whosoever believeth in him should not perish, but have everlasting life"[12]

Both God and man will do things for love that will never be done for any other reason. This truth was powerfully taught to me through an experience shared with me by my aunt.

---

[9] https://en.wikipedia.org/wiki/Sinners_in_the_Hands_of_an_Angry_God

[10] Moses 7:24-37

[11] Moses 7:37

[12] John 3:16

Charity Never Faileth

Several years ago I was visiting my aunt's home and she shared with me several worn newspaper clippings. Their fragile nature told of their age and the many times they have been unfolded, read, re-folded and carefully tucked away. The clippings told of the death of two young boys who had been hit and killed by a freight train.

"Who were the boys?" I asked my aunt.

"They were my brothers," she said. "I was just a baby then."

She then shared with me what had happened. It was a summer day in Muldrow, a small town in the northeast corner of Oklahoma. Wesley Butcher, my aunt's father, had taken his three sons to "dip cattle". Cattle dipping was a procedure where the livestock was walked through long vats of insecticide to kill and repel ticks that caused cattle tick fever. The young boys enjoyed working with their father and were close in age. Vernal was ten years old, Leonard was eight and Orville was six.

The early morning chore had gone well so that by 9 a.m. the father and boys were driving their cattle back home. They walked along the dirt road that ran parallel to the Missouri Pacific railroad tracks. Still full of energy the boys ran ahead, playing along the way.

Some distance ahead of their father the three brothers began walking on a trestle bridge over which the railroad tracks ran. The boys were only partially across when they heard the whistle of a quickly approaching freight train. Since the trestle was no more than 10 feet above the ground, the father called to the boys to jump.

Vernal, the oldest, was first to jump. But as Leonard prepared to jump he heard the youngest cry out. He turned and saw that Orville's foot was caught in a cattle guard. Leonard turned and worked frantically to free his little brother. As the train whistle screamed, both father and Vernal raced to reach the two brothers. Neither would make it in time. Leonard, realizing he would not be able to free his younger brother, simply threw his arms around him and both were struck by the oncoming train.

When their father saw the critical injuries of his sons he quickly flagged a passing motorist. The two boys were placed in the vehicle and hurried to a hospital in Fort Smith, Arkansas, about 13 miles away. Orville died within minutes of being placed in the car. Leonard died later that evening in the hospital.

To seal the act of love, the two boys were buried in the same grave.

One of the newspaper clippings I read was an editorial from *Southwest American*, a local newspaper:

> The heroism of eight-year-old Leonard Butcher, a farmer's boy of Muldrow, is a wonderful thing to think about. . . . In that instant when Leonard looked back and saw his baby brother stumbling and falling in the path of the engine, Leonard was no longer a child, a farmer's boy, driving cattle down a dusty road. He became a man-sized hero fired with that spirit of self-sacrifice which has made life worth living . . . .
>
> Leonard turned in the face of death, and was hurled into eternity with his baby brother in his arms; his whole mind and heart intent on that very act which the Christian world bases its hope of eternity – giving his life that another might live.[13]

The Power of Perfect Love

What brings a boy to throw his arms around his brother in the face of certain death? The scriptures describe this level of love as charity, "the pure love of Christ".[14] It is more powerful than

---

[13] Copy of the clipping in the author's possession.

[14] Moroni 7:47

pain, stronger than fear, and undefeated in death. It "never faileth".[15]

In this story, we can find a powerful similitude of the Savior's atonement. Like Orville, we are the ones who are trapped, unable to free ourselves from the oncoming effects of sin and death. But an older Brother ran to our rescue. Without sin, He was free to jump from the path of the oncoming pain. Instead, He threw His arms around us and took the awful blow.

This is the depth of love that lies at the very center of the redeeming work of the Father and Son. It is far and away the most powerful force in the universe. Neither hate nor evil will ever defeat it because neither is willing to climb to the same heights nor rescue at the same depths.

The Power of Daily Repentance

We can sometimes slip into the thinking that repentance is primarily for those involved in more serious sins. President Russell M. Nelson, 17th president of the Church, has taught that repentance is a daily affair for all of us:

> Nothing is more liberating, more ennobling, or more crucial to our individual progression than is a regular, daily focus on repentance. Repentance is not an event; it is a process. It is the key to happiness and peace of mind. When coupled with faith, repentance opens our access to the power of the Atonement of Jesus Christ.
>
> Whether you are diligently moving along the covenant path, have slipped or stepped from the covenant path, or can't even see the path from where you are now, I plead with you to repent. Experience the strengthening power of daily repentance—of doing and being a little better each day.

---

[15] Moroni 7:46

When we choose to repent, we choose to change! We allow the Savior to transform us into the best version of ourselves. We choose to grow spiritually and receive joy—the joy of redemption in Him. When we choose to repent, we choose to become more like Jesus Christ![16]

Faith Unto Repentance

All of us are sinners. But our Father, in His mercy and grace, has provided the means by which we can become clean and spotless through the atonement of His loving Son. All who exercise "faith unto repentance" will find a Father who runs to welcome them home and a Brother who "encircles them in the arms of safety".[17]

---

[16] Ensign, May 2019

[17] Alma 34:15-16

Sabbath

*"The Lord has given the Sabbath day for your benefit
and has commanded you to keep it holy. Many activities
are appropriate for the Sabbath. Bear in mind, however,
that Sunday is not a holiday. Sunday is a holy day."*
- President Thomas S. Monson[1]

T he purposes and guidelines regarding the Sabbath day can
sometimes be confusing. The Lord commanded us to *cease*
working and to *rest* on the Sabbath.[2] But what about activities
like fishing or golfing? Are those considered *working*? And what
about the bishop? Sunday can be the busiest day of the week
for him. Is that considered *resting*?

---

[1] *Ensign*, Nov. 1990

[2] Exodus 20:8-11

There is an object lesson I once saw that greatly enlarged my understanding of the purpose of the Sabbath. The teacher took a 25-foot string and stretched it across the floor at the front of the classroom. He then invited a volunteer to come forward and walk along the string with his eyes closed. After 25 feet the person was no longer walking on the string. The teacher asked, "If the string were a mile long, how far off of the string could you be by the time you reached the end?" The person admitted he would end up quite a distance away from the string.

Then the teacher asked the volunteer to walk along the string again. This time, however, the volunteer was allowed to open his eyes every seventh step and readjust his feet back onto the string. After 25 feet he was still on the string. The teacher then asked, "If this string were a mile long and you could open your eyes every seventh step, how far off of the string would you be at the end of the mile?" His answer: "No more than a couple of inches."

Every seven days the Lord gives us a special day to open our spiritual eyes and readjust ourselves back onto the straight and narrow. Those who truly keep the Sabbath holy will never wander far from the path that leads back to the Father.

The Meaning of Sabbath

The word *Sabbath* literally means *to cease*. The Lord is asking us to cease from certain activities on His holy day. Many activities may not be what we would consider as *work* but they distract from the real purpose of the Sabbath – drawing closer to our Heavenly Father.

I believe Isaiah gives some of the best guidelines for determining what activities are most appropriate for the Sabbath:

> If thou turn thy foot from the Sabbath, from doing thy pleasure on my holy day; and call the Sabbath a delight, the holy of the Lord, honorable; and shalt honour him, not doing thine own ways, nor finding thine own pleasure, nor speaking thine own words.

> Then shalt thou delight thyself in the Lord; and I will cause thee to ride upon the high places of the earth, and feed thee with the heritage of Jacob thy father: for the mouth of the Lord hath spoken it.[3]

The Sabbath is the Lord's Day. Our focus should be to make it a *holy day*. It is a day to honor God, to become spiritually refreshed and strengthened by drawing closer to Him. In the previous verses the Lord gives several promises to those who honor the Sabbath:

1. **Delight in the Lord** – They will come to love the peace and spirituality of that day.

2. **Ride the high places** – The prophets of old would climb to high places to draw close to God and be taught by His Spirit. True Sabbath observance will draw us closer to God and allow a greater influence of His Spirit to guide our lives.

3. **Receive the heritage of Jacob** – One meaning of the word *heritage* is *inheritance*. Doctrine and Covenants 132:37 tells us that Jacob has inherited his exaltation. The Sabbath is designed to help us receive the same.

A One-Month Experiment

I once asked a group of my students to select a principle of the gospel they wanted to improve in their lives. I challenged them to work on it for one month and then report back on what happened. Several of my students decided to improve their efforts in keeping the Sabbath day holy. Here's what two of them experienced.

---

[3] Isaiah 58:13-14

"I Felt Peaceful and Pleased"

"The challenge of keeping the Sabbath Day holy was a bit more difficult than I had expected. I was pretty good at not spending money on Sundays, but I would always watch television just to give me something to do. I knew there were better, more productive things to do with my time. So I sat down and made a list of constructive things I could do on Sundays: writing in my journal, studying the scriptures, praying, visiting the sick, visiting with my family, writing letters to friends and missionaries.

"On the following Sunday, I woke up and did my usual routine of getting ready for church. After church, instead of plopping down in front of the television, I began doing things on my list. I felt very peaceful and pleased with what I had accomplished.

"As a result of this experience, I have discovered a greater closeness to my Heavenly Father and a better focus for my life."

"The Lord Kept His Promise"

"I received a scholarship to attend college and needed to maintain a 3.7 grade point average in order to keep it. I had been going out with friends on Fridays and Saturdays, leaving only Sundays to do my homework. Prior to that time Sundays had been very enjoyable for me. I would take a nap, read my scriptures and visit with my family. But it got to the point where I no longer had time for those things. I started hating Sundays because of the stress and pressure of homework. My grades started slipping and I was stressing out 'big time'.

"Then I realized it wasn't Sunday that I hated. It was the fact that I didn't have a day of rest anymore. I decided to make a commitment to the Lord that I would no longer do homework on Sunday. I asked Him to please help me make time on the other days to do my homework and to help me remember the things I studied.

"This really was an eye-opening experience for me. I worked hard on my studying, but I know the Lord helped me. I've

110

received an "A" on every test since making the commitment. More important than the grade is the fact that my Sundays are back to how they used to be. I love and look forward to Sundays again. The rest and the peace I receive on that day always help me to make it through the week and give me something to look forward to.

"This experience has also strengthened my testimony. I know the scripture in Doctrine and Covenants 82:10 is true: 'I, the Lord, am bound when ye do what I say; but when ye do not what I say, ye have no promise.' I kept my part of the promise and the Lord kept His."

A Day of Delight

There are so many things that can distract us from fully enjoying the blessings of the Sabbath. These two girls exercised faith in setting aside their own pleasures. And in return, they discovered how the Sabbath can truly be a day of peace, a day of rest, a day of delight.

17

Testimony

*"And he had hoped to shake me from the faith,
notwithstanding the many revelations and the many
things which I had seen concerning these things . . .
wherefore, I could not be shaken."*[1]

A s a seminary teacher I had the opportunity to attend weekly in-service training. Most sessions proved rewarding and worth the time spent. But there was one in-service that had not only a powerful effect on my teaching but on my personal life as well.

On that afternoon the training was being held at a different seminary. I had arrived a little early and was taking advantage

---

[1] Jacob 7:5

of the time by walking through several classes to get some ideas for my own classroom.

As I walked into Ken Miller's room I found him preparing the next day's lesson. He had an illustration on the chalkboard that caught my eye. The drawing was a simple stick figure of a man with three arrows pointing to it. The first arrow pointed to the stick figure's head with the word "HEAD" next to the arrow. The second arrow pointed to the area of the stick figure's chest with the word "HEART" next to it. And the third pointed to the stick figure's hand with the word "HAND" next to it. Above the stick figure in bold lettering were the words "THREE KINDS OF TESTIMONY".

I paused and asked Ken, "Three kinds of testimony? I don't think I've ever heard of that."

He smiled and said, "I believe there are three kinds of testimony. The testimony of the head, the testimony of the heart and the testimony of the hand."

I was intrigued. I asked him to explain.

"The testimony of the heart is the one most people are familiar with," Ken began. "It's the testimony where the Holy Ghost confirms the truth to your heart. That kind of testimony is spoken of by the prophet Moroni in Moroni 10:3-5. It's also spoken of by the Savior when He asked His disciples:

Whom do men say that I the Son of man am?

And they said, Some say that thou art John the Baptist: some, Elias; and others, Jeremias, or one of the prophets.

He saith unto them, But whom say ye that I am?

And Simon Peter answered and said, Thou art the Christ, the Son of the living God.

And Jesus answered and said unto him, Blessed art thou, Simon Bar-jona: for flesh and blood hath not revealed it unto thee, but my Father which is in heaven.[2]

"That makes sense," I said. "How about the other two?"

"The testimony of the hand is the witness that comes when we live a principle and see the promised blessings come to pass. We pay our tithing and we see the windows of heaven open. We ask our Father in prayer and we receive an answer. The Savior spoke of that kind of testimony when He said, 'My doctrine is not mine, but his that sent me. If any man will do his will, he shall know of the doctrine, whether it be of God, or whether I speak of myself.'[3]

"I like it," I said. "And the third?"

"The testimony of the head is when you study the doctrines and principles of the gospel in the scriptures and discover that they are in harmony with what our church teaches. For example, one of the doctrines taught in the Church of Jesus Christ of Latter-Day Saints is baptism for the dead. Paul testified of that doctrine in 1 Corinthian 15:29. Another example is the doctrine of temples. There were temples in both the Old and New Testament. The true Church of Jesus Christ will have temples."

Then he added, "I believe every member of the Church of Jesus Christ of Latter-Day Saints should have all three kinds of testimony. A three-legged stool is much more solid and stable than a one or two-legged stool."

I have never forgotten that experience. And it helped explain a humbling experience I had in the mission field years earlier.

The Seventh-day Adventist Minister

I served in the German Central Mission from 1972 to 1974. It was a wonderful yet challenging experience. In my mission, the missionaries spent most of the day – every day – knocking on

---

[2] Matthew 16:15-17

[3] John 7:16-17

doors. Teaching a discussion to someone was not a frequent experience.

I had been in the mission field about six months when my companion, Elder Greg Bates, and I knocked on the door of a woman who identified herself as Seventh-day Adventist. She kindly told us she had no interest in hearing our message but said her minister loved to talk with LDS missionaries. She gave us his phone number in case we were interested. We were! It would mean we would be able to teach someone rather than spending another evening knocking on unwelcoming doors.

We called and set up an appointment with the minister. He sounded warm and friendly. We were excited! And though we were a little nervous to be meeting with a minister we felt we could adequately defend the faith.

We were wrong.

A day or so later we arrived at his apartment where he and his wife warmly invited us inside. They were kind, friendly and sincere. After a few minutes of pleasant conversation we began to discuss religion. He asked if members of the Church of Jesus Christ of Latter-Day Saints believe in the Bible. We told him we do, although we believe there are passages that have not been translated correctly.

Then he surprised us. He asked us to share with him and his wife the experience of Joseph Smith's first vision. We sensed that he was going somewhere with his request. We began sharing how Joseph Smith was confused about religion and came across the promise found in James 1:5. We explained how Joseph went to a grove of trees and began offering up a prayer to God when he was attacked by Satan. We described how Joseph was delivered from the Destroyer when a pillar of light descended from heaven. In the light were two glorious Beings standing above him in the air.

He stopped us.

"Two Beings?" he asked.

That caught us off guard a bit. "Yes, two Beings."

"Are you sure there wasn't just one?" he questioned.

Again, that struck us as odd.

"No, there were two."

"Who were they?" he asked.

"One was God the Father and the other was Jesus Christ, His Son."

We realized the minister was trying to make a point so we paused.

"Let me tell you what concerns me about this young man's story," he said. "You stated that your church believes in the Bible. The Bible teaches that no one has ever been allowed to see God the Father."

He opened his Bible to John 1:18 and asked us to read: "No man hath seen God at any time; the only begotten Son, which is in the bosom of the Father, he hath declared him."

"The apostle John is clearly stating that no mortal man has seen God," he said.

He then opened to John 6:46 and again invited us to read: "Not that any man hath seen the Father, save he which is of God, he hath seen the Father."

"Only Jesus is of God," he said. "He's seen the Father. But according to the Bible, which you said your church believes, no mortal man has seen Him. Your boy prophet is claiming an experience that no previous prophet has ever claimed."

Elder Bates reminded the minister that Moses had seen God face to face.[4]

"That's correct," he said. "But was that Jehovah the Son or Elohim the Father?"

We admitted it was Jehovah.

---

[4] Exodus 33:11

"You see if your boy prophet would have claimed to have seen Jehovah or Jesus Christ that would have been believable. But he's saying he saw both the Father and the Son. And the Bible says no mortal except Jesus has seen the Father."

Elder Bates and I looked at each other. Neither of us had an answer.

Nor did we have answers for the additional ten or so questions he asked us. Each question stumped and stupefied us. The minister was never rude or offensive. But he knew the scriptures MUCH better than we did. And because of that, we could not defend the faith.

With heads hanging we headed toward the front door. Our host shook our hands and kindly thanked us for coming. He said he would be willing to talk with us anytime. He offered to show us answers in his church if we could not find answers in our own.

By now my spiritual world had lost its equilibrium. It didn't make sense what had just happened. I had received a strong witness of both Jesus Christ and Joseph Smith before my mission. I had found peace and happiness in living the teachings of the restored Gospel. I believed them to be true. But what I believed no longer seemed to be in harmony with what the Bible taught. I was deeply troubled, as was my companion. We returned to our apartment and poured out our hearts to Heavenly Father for answers.

Early the next morning we again pleaded for heavenly help and then sprang into the scriptures. We were no longer reading. We began searching.

Over the next few weeks, we found answers to all of the minister's questions. We discovered that the Bible testifies that mortal man can and has seen the Father. In the Sermon on the Mount Jesus taught that such was possible when He stated that the pure in heart shall see God.[5] Jesus would later testify that

---

[5] Matthew 5:8

the Son would reveal the Father to those who are faithful.[6] Even more significant is the account of Stephen who, prior to being stoned, looked into the heavens and saw Jesus standing on the right hand of God.[7]

Years later I decided to read the New Testament and put an asterisk each time I found a doctrine or teaching that coincided with the teachings of the restored Gospel. It was an amazing journey that greatly strengthened my "testimony of the head". These are but a few of the things I discovered:

- Jesus Christ called twelve apostles and gave them the power to cast out devils and heal the sick. Look for a church that has twelve apostles who have been given power to act in His name.[8]

- The apostle Peter spoke of the Lord instigating the work for the dead.[9] Search for a church that seeks to save those who have long since died.

- The apostle Paul stated that he knew a man who saw the third heaven. The true church should have doctrine that teaches of three heavens.[10]

- Paul and many others referred to the members of the church as Saints.[11]

- The apostle James taught: "Is any sick among you? let him call for the elders of the church; and let them pray over him, anointing him with oil in the name of Lord."[12] The true church of Jesus Christ will have elders who

---

[6] Matthew 11:27

[7] Acts 7:55-56

[8] Matthew 10:1

[9] 1 Peter 3:18-20, 1 Peter 4:6

[10] 2 Corinthians 12:2

[11] Ephesians 2:19-20 and in more than 90 additional scriptures

[12] James 5:14

have the power and authority to anoint and bless the sick.

I consider the experience with the minister to be a great blessing in my life. It led me to discover the difference between reading and searching the scriptures. It opened the door to feasting upon the scriptures in a way I had not previously experienced. And it launched the beginning of a testimony of the head that has strengthened my testimony ever since.

The Winds Are Increasing

All of us will face numerous times when our testimony will be challenged. The winds of opposition are increasing. Those who do not have deep roots of testimony will topple. President Heber C. Kimball (1801 – 1868), a member of the Quorum of the Twelve Apostles and counselor to Brigham Young in the First Presidency, gave a prophecy that is clearly coming to pass:

> This Church has before it many close places through which it will have to pass before the work of God is crowned with glory. The difficulties will be of such a character that the man or woman who does not possess a personal knowledge or witness will fall. If you have not got this testimony, you must live right and call upon the Lord, and cease not until you obtain it.
>
> Remember these sayings: The time will come when no man or woman will be able to endure on borrowed light. Each will have to be guided by the light within themselves.[13]

A powerful example of this was shared in a priesthood meeting I attended. Adam Allred, a member of my ward, shared with us a 'trial of testimony' he faced while preparing to serve a mission.

---

[13] *Life of Heber C. Kimball*, by Orson F Whitney, 450

"My Mind Was Opened and I Could See"

"I always knew I would go on a mission. I had been brought up in a family that earnestly strived to live the gospel of Jesus Christ. I shared the conviction of my parents and the prophet that every worthy young man should serve a mission. I felt that I had a testimony. But as my 19th birthday drew near the circumstances in my life began to change drastically.

"My father was a military man and the summer I was turning 19 we learned he was to be transferred from our home in Derby, Kansas to Washington D.C. The transfer took place two months before my birthday. All of my friends, most of them nonmembers, and the young love of my life (also a nonmember) were in Kansas. I elected to stay and live with a good friend rather than move with my parents.

"My friend and his family showed me great kindness and love but their faith was firm in a Christian denomination that was strongly anti-Mormon. In their misguided zeal and concern, they did all they could to talk me out of going on a mission.

"To make things worse my girlfriend and her family were also members of a church with anti-Mormon feelings. A day didn't go by that I wasn't bombarded with some sort of anti-Mormon conversation or literature. I stood up for the Church in all of these instances but was unprepared and outnumbered. Secretly my resolve to serve a mission was crumbling. I was no longer certain of anything. And I was very much alone. My family was hundreds of miles away. My few LDS friends were either away on missions or wandering down their own paths of misty darkness.

"What was infinitely worse was that I was gradually separating myself more and more from the Spirit. I began to see the perceived advantages of not going on a mission. I didn't want to leave my girlfriend, my buddies, or my job. Life seemed like it was just really starting for me and now the prospect of a mission seemed too inconvenient and too demanding. A few months prior I would have been completely shocked that I would have even entertained such notions. But despite the adversity I faced, there was still a spark that seemed to dispel the darkness when I was alone and had time to think.

"One particular night I went to pick up my girlfriend for a date. As I was waiting in her living room I was confronted with a calculated presentation of anti-Mormon propaganda from her mother and father. For the rest of the night, I was deeply troubled. What they had said wasn't new but it seemed to darken the little spark inside me.

"After I dropped her off and returned home I was weary and confused. Upon my arrival, I was greeted by my friend's mother. She asked if she could talk to me though I was desperate to retire for the evening. She proceeded to present me with a wide variety of 'evidence' that attacked the LDS faith. Much of what she said echoed what my girlfriend's parents had told me earlier in the evening: Joseph Smith was a false prophet and the Bible was the only word of God.

"After she finished I hurried to my room with a shaken testimony. My little spark needed fuel or it would be gone forever. I dropped to my knees and poured out my whole soul in prayer. I pleaded with the Lord to have mercy on me and to give me some sort of direction. I was drowning.

"When I finished I felt only moderately better. I felt prompted to open my scriptures and read. I flipped randomly to 2 Nephi 29. I was not familiar with the chapter. But as I read, something peculiar and amazing happened. My mind was opened and I could see. Everything that I had been dealing with the last few weeks seemed to be answered in that chapter. For the first time in my life, I knew that I was receiving an answer to my prayer. It was more than a quiet whisper. I felt like I was burning up inside as I read: 'Thou fool that shall say, A Bible, we have got a Bible, and we need no more Bible'.[14]

"I had started reading the chapter silently but by the end of the chapter I was almost yelling out the words. All the confusion and fear were dispelled and I could clearly see how close I had

---

[14] 2 Nephi 29:6

come to losing my soul to the adversary. All the countless hours of anti-Mormon attacks were destroyed by a few precious moments with the Spirit of God.

"From that day on I no longer prayed to know if I should go on a mission, but for the strength to go. I prayed in faith, knowing that the Lord would bless me, just like Nephi, to accomplish all that He commanded me.

"A few months and a few small miracles later (miracles always follow those who have faith) I turned in my papers to go on my mission. It was still difficult pulling away from my friends and the girl that I cared so much for, but the Lord sustained me.

"And speaking of miracles, not only did several of my friends join the church while I was on my mission but so did my girlfriend."[15]

Gaining and Maintaining a Testimony

Testimonies are not born in a day. They take faith, effort and time. And testimonies, like tender plants, must continually receive nourishment if they are to grow and mature. The prophet Alma gave a promise to all earnest seekers of truth:

But if ye will nourish the word, yea, nourish the tree as it beginneth to grow, by your faith with great diligence and with patience, looking forward to the fruit thereof, it shall take root; and behold it shall be a tree springing up unto everlasting life.[16]

---

[15] This story is in the author's possession.

[16] Alma 32:41

18

Tithing

*"Pay your tithes and offerings out of honesty and
integrity because they are God's rightful due. Surely one
of the most piercing lines in all of scripture is Jehovah's
thundering inquiry, "Will a man rob God?"*
- Elder Jeffrey R. Holland[1]

As a bishop, I always enjoyed tithing settlement. Though it
puts a little additional time demands on the bishop, it is a
wonderful opportunity to meet with the Saints and be
strengthened by their faith. During the five years I served I had
the opportunity to hear the tithing declaration of many faithful
members. But there is one interview I will never forget.

A mother came with her children to declare their tithing
faithfulness. Before going into my office she pulled me aside

---

[1] *Ensign*, November 2001

and told me that her six-year-old son, Tanner, refused to pay his tithing. She asked me if I could somehow help him understand the importance of this commandment. I agreed.

As the family sat down in my office I proceeded to ask each of them if they were faithful tithe payers. Each, in turn, nodded their head. Until I reached Tanner.

"Tanner, did you pay a full tithing this year?"

Tanner looked at the floor and said with a scowl, "No."

"How come?" I gently asked.

"Because I don't want to," he said.

"Well, the Lord doesn't force anyone to pay tithing. But do you know what He calls people who won't pay their tithing?"

Suddenly I had Tanner's interest. The scowl left. He looked at me, not sure he wanted to know.

I opened my Bible, turned to the third chapter of Malachi and read, "Will a man rob God? Yet ye have robbed me. But ye say, Wherein have we robbed thee? In tithes and offerings."[2]

I looked up and said, "The Lord considers us thieves and robbers when we don't pay our tithing." Tanner was listening intently. Then I gently added, "It's totally up to you whether or not you pay tithing. But I am always glad to pay my tithing. It's one way I can show Heavenly Father and Jesus that I love them and am thankful for my many blessings. I certainly would never want to steal from them."

I stood, thanked them for coming and they left.

Later that night I received a phone call. The mother was on the phone. "Bishop," she said, "Tanner would like to speak to you. Do you have another minute?" I told her I would love to talk with Tanner. She handed him the phone and I heard a little voice say, "Hi, Bishop. I want to pay my tithing."

---

[2] Malachi 3:8

"Tanner, that's great! What made you change your mind?"

He quietly responded, "I don't want to steal from Jesus."

I told him how pleased Heavenly Father would be with him. I hung up the phone, grateful for his desire to be honest with the Lord.

Jesus Christ makes a marvelous promise to all faithful tithe payers. He pledges to "open you the windows of heaven, and pour you out a blessing, that there shall not be room enough to receive it."[3] One of the members of my stake shared with me how the Lord fulfilled that promise to her and her sister.

A Testimony of Tithing

"Before moving to Utah to attend school, my sister Aarika and I were living at home and working to save for our education. When we received our paychecks we noticed there would be enough to pay for the apartment we would be renting. But if we paid our tithing on that money we wouldn't have enough to pay rent. We both decided to pay our tithing first and trust that the Lord would help us.

"We prayed and fasted for the Lord to guide and help us with our situation. A few days later I got online to see how much I had left in my bank account. I noticed that the balance of my account had increased! I was confused and thought something was wrong. I checked all the transactions and learned I had been given a $400.00 deposit from the college we would be attending. I screamed and yelled for Aarika to come downstairs. I showed her my account and then told her to check her account. Her account showed the same – a $400.00 deposit from the college. We were jumping for joy!

"Not only did the Lord provide us with enough money to pay for rent, but He provided us with more than we needed! We paid our rent on time and had extra money for other

---

[3] Malachi 3:10

necessities. We had exercised our faith in the Lord's promises and He had opened the windows of heaven."[4]

Faith, Not Finance

I once heard a ward member say he couldn't explain how tithing works. "It doesn't make sense financially. You shouldn't be able to give your money away and then have more. But one way or the other, the Lord repays you – with interest."

The foundation for paying tithing is not based on finance. It is based on faith.

---

[4] Story in the author's possession

19

The Word of Wisdom

"I bear witness that this revelation is a powerful protection to all members of the Church, particularly to you, the youth of the Church, as you face a life full of so many troubles and danger and uncertainties."
– President Boyd K. Packer[1]

Imagine that you've just purchased an expensive car. You've dreamed of owning this car. You've been working hard and saving money for what seems like forever. You finally have enough to write the check and drive home in this beautiful vehicle.

---

[1] *Ensign*, May 1996

The first thing you do is wash it and wax it. Then you take it for a drive around the neighborhood. You show it to your friends. They're jealous! They know you've got yourself a 'sweet ride'.

After several days you run low on gas. You go to a gas station and are just ready to tank up when someone steps from the shadows and calls to you. You realize it's one of your friends. He waves you over and tells you that he has something much more powerful than gas to put in your tank. He says the fuel he has will make your car run better and faster. He shows you a five-gallon container and tells you he's willing to sell it to you for a great price. Would you buy it and pour it in the tank of your expensive new car?

I'm guessing you wouldn't.

This imaginary scenario is played out in real life thousands of times each day as people throughout the world are encouraged by advertisers, friends, and peers to put tobacco, drugs, and alcohol into their bodies. It may surprise you that many people are more careful about what they put into their cars than what they put into their bodies. And cars are replaceable! Try getting yourself another body! No replacements or trade-ins until the resurrection.

A Revelation from God

Our body is an amazing machine designed for us by the Lord. He has given us special guidelines so we know which types of *fuel* make it run best and what will damage it. His counsel is found in Doctrine and Covenants 89 and is known as the Word of Wisdom. This revelation was given to the Prophet Joseph Smith more than a hundred years before scientists knew the dangers of tobacco, alcohol, tea, and coffee. It was given long before scientists confirmed the foods the Lord says are good for our bodies. Everything in that revelation – everything! – has now been verified by modern research. What a witness to the world that Joseph Smith was a prophet of God!

This revelation contains at least three promises to those who follow the Lord's counsel:

1. **Health** (verses 18, 20) – Even though the revelation does not promise perfect health, those who follow this principle will be healthier and stronger.

2. **Wisdom and great treasures of knowledge** (verse 19) – Powerful truths and understanding can come through the Holy Ghost.[2] Those who keep their minds and bodies free from damaging substances are much more susceptible to the Spirit's influence.

3. **The destroying angel shall pass them by** (verse 21) – President Boyd K. Packer (1924 – 2015), president of the Quorum of the Twelve Apostles, taught that "it is not from mortal death that we shall be spared in such a passover if we walk in obedience to these commandments, for each of us in time shall die. But there is spiritual death which you need not suffer. If you are obedient, that spiritual death will pass over you."[3]

A Personal Gift from God

President Russell M. Nelson, 17th president of the Church, has counseled:

When we understand our nature and our purpose on earth and that our bodies are physical temples of God, we will realize that it is sacrilege to let anything enter that might defile the body. It is truly irreverent to let even the gaze of our precious eyesight or the sensors of our touch or hearing supply the brain with memories that are unclean or unworthy. We will cherish our chastity and avoid "foolish and hurtful lusts, which drown [us] in destruction and perdition."[4] We will "flee

---

[2] 1 Nephi 10:19, Moroni 10:5

[3] *Ensign*, May 1996

[4] 1 Timothy 6:9

these things; and follow after righteousness, godliness, faith, love, patience, [and] meekness"[5] – traits that edify the whole soul.

Substances such as alcohol, tobacco, and harmful drugs are forbidden by the Lord. We have similarly been warned about the evils of pornography and unclean thoughts. Appetites for these degrading forces can become addictive. In time, physical or mental addictions enslave both the body and the spirit. Repentance from such shackles should be accomplished in this life while we still have the aid of a mortal body to help us develop self-mastery.

Our Creator put appetites in our bodies to perpetuate the human race and fulfill His great plan of happiness. Thus, we have appetites for food, for water, and for love.

Satan knows the power of our appetites. So, he tempts us to eat things we should not eat, to drink things we should not drink, and to desecrate the most intimate expressions of love by employing them outside the bounds of marriage.

When we truly know our divine nature, we will want to control such appetites. And we will focus our eyes on sights, our ears on sounds, and our minds on thoughts that are a credit to our physical creation as a temple of God. In daily prayer, we will gratefully acknowledge Him as our Creator and thank Him for the magnificence of our own physical temple. We will care for it and cherish it as our own personal gift from God.[6]

---

[5] 1 Timothy 6:11

[6] New Era, August 2019

Clarification on Certain Substances

In recent publications[7], Church leaders have provided clarification on several substances that are also prohibited by the Word of Wisdom. These include vaping or e-cigarettes, green tea, and coffee-based products. Our leaders have also cautioned that substances such as marijuana and opioids should be used only for medicinal purposes as prescribed by a competent physician.

"I Made Up My Mind"

As a young boy, President Spencer W. Kimball (1895 – 1985), 12th president of the Church, made a decision about the Word of Wisdom that had a powerful effect on his life:

> When I was a little boy...I heard my teachers tell me over and over: "We do not drink; we do not smoke; we do not drink tea or coffee..."
>
> Then as I was out alone, milking the cows, or putting up the hay, I had time to think. I mulled it over in my mind and made this decision: "I, Spencer Kimball, will never taste any form of liquor. I, Spencer Kimball, will never touch tobacco. I will never drink coffee, nor will I ever touch tea—not because I can explain why I shouldn't, except that the Lord said not to." He said those things were an abomination. There are many other things that are, too, that are not in the Word of Wisdom. But I made up my mind.
>
> That's the point I am trying to make. I made up my mind then, as a little boy; "I will never touch those things." And so, having made up my mind, it was easy to follow it, and I did not yield. There were many temptations that came along, but I did not even analyze it; I did not stop and measure it and say, "Well, shall I or

---

[7] *New Era*, August 2019

shall I not?" I always said to myself: "But I made up my mind I would not. Therefore, I do not."

I want to just say that I will soon go into another year and that I have never tasted tea, nor coffee, nor tobacco, nor liquor of any kind, nor drugs. Now that may sound very presumptuous and boasting to you, but I am only trying to make this point: that if every boy and girl—as he or she begins to grow a little more mature and becomes a little more independent of his friends and his family and all—if every boy and girl would make up his or her mind, I will not yield, then no matter what the temptation is: I made up my mind. That's settled.[8]

Have you made that decision yet? Rand Packer shares a wonderful story about one of his friends who had.

"If Any of You Are Men"

"At the age of fourteen several friends and I were headed on a campout to the mountains of Utah's west desert. We were traveling on a dark, winding road in the back of an old open-bed fire truck when one of my friends reached into his pack and pulled out a can of beer. Everyone went silent as he popped the lid and held it high towards the sky. 'If any of you are men,' he bellowed, 'you'll have a drink with me!' The can quickly went to his lips as he drew a large swallow from the can. He exhaled with gusto and passed it to the boy next to him.

"All eyes were now on the can as the second boy received it into his waiting hand. In an instant, the can was to his lips as he took a swig with great bravado in front of us all.

"As the can moved in my direction my mind sprinted for some quick answer, some cool response that would rescue me. I knew what was right and wrong. I knew what the Word of Wisdom said. I knew the story of young Joseph Smith needing to have

---

[8] *Church News*, October 4, 1975

infected bone removed from his leg and his refusing the doctors' suggestion to drink liquor to endure the pain.

"These things were racing in my mind as the can found its way to the third boy, a little guy on his very first campout. He had not come to break a covenant or to be tempted. He thought he was just going camping. As he held the can I could sense the frantic thoughts going on in his own mind. All eyes were upon him, almost demanding that he drink as the others had. I could almost hear his pleading cries for his mother to come and save him, but she was nowhere to be found. Try as he did, he could not handle the pressure. He closed his eyes, nervously brought the can to his mouth and let some trickle down his throat.

"He hurriedly passed the can to Rick, my friend, my buddy, my example. 'Rick,' I thought, 'if you take one sip of that I'm going to slug you so hard!' Rick held the can out in front of us. He looked at me and I looked at him. We both looked at the can he was holding. Then we looked at thirteen faces waiting anxiously.

"My heart was pounding with the realization that I was next in the circle. My mind was absolutely empty as to how I was going to wiggle out of this one gracefully. I knew that if I didn't take a drink they would bury me up to my neck in the foothills and let the ants play tag through my nose and ears.

"For a long moment, Rick just stared at the can of beer. And then very casually he took it and put it between his knees. He reached into his pack, fished around for something and then pulled it out. It was the most beautiful purple thing I had ever seen. He raised it to heaven where all could see.

"'If any of you are men,' Rick yelled as he raised the purple can, 'you'll have a drink of grape soda with me!'

"Rick popped the lid, brought it to his lips with authority, swigged down the purple pop and then passed it back in the other direction.

"The kid on the other side of Rick now found himself holding the purple can. He quickly took a drink and passed it to the boy on the other side of him. As they were enjoying the purple soda,

Rick reached down, grabbed the can of beer and heaved it as far as he could. I shall never forget seeing that frothing can spin through the air as it descended into the gully below.

"It just takes one person to stand up in a world of darkness and show forth a little light. Just as surely as a single light bulb can illuminate the darkest of rooms, so a single individual can chase away the engulfing darkness.

"God bless you, Rick, for turning on the light for all of us."[9]

Despite tremendous peer pressure, a young man trusts the Lord's counsel to keep the Word of Wisdom. *That's faith!*

---

[9] Story in possession of the author

True to the Faith

"True, today is a new day with new trials, new troubles, and new temptations, but hundreds of thousands of Latter-day Saint youth strive constantly and serve diligently, true to the faith, as their counterparts of earlier years so nobly did."
- President Thomas S. Monson[1]

I close the book with a final story that I hope will inspire you as much as it does me. It is told by President Spencer W. Kimball (1895 – 1995), twelfth president of the Church.

---

[1] *Ensign*, February 1997

"I Gritted My Teeth"

"When I was a youngster, a stirring challenge came to me that moved me not a little. I cannot remember who issued the challenge nor under what circumstances it came. I remember only that it struck me like a 'bolt out of the blue heavens.' The unknown voice postulated:

> The "Mormon Church" has stood its ground for the first two generations—but wait till the third and fourth and succeeding generations come along! The first generation fired with a new religion developed a great enthusiasm for it. Surrounded with bitterness, calumny of a hostile world, persecuted "from pillar to post," they were forced to huddle together for survival. There was good reason to expect they would live and die faithful to their espoused cause.
>
> The second generation came along born to enthusiasts, zealots, devotees. They were born to men and women who had developed great faith, were inured to hardships and sacrifices for their faith. They inherited from their parents and soaked up from religious homes the stuff of which the faithful are made. They had full reservoirs of strength and faith upon which to draw.
>
> But wait till the third and fourth generations come along,' said the cynical voice. 'The fire will have gone out—the devotion will have been diluted—the sacrifice will have been nullified—the world will have hovered over them and surrounded them and eroded them—the faith will have been expended and the religious fervor leaked out.'

That day I realized that I was a member of the third generation. That day I clenched my growing fists. I gritted my teeth and made a firm commitment to myself that here was one 'third generation' who would not fulfill that dire prediction."[2]

The Faithful of Our Day

You and I are now several generations beyond that third generation. Yes, there are some who have allowed their faith to fade. Yes, there are others in whom the fire has gone out. However, there are many whose faith has not and will not falter. Nephi saw our day in vision and spoke of these faithful Saints:

> And it came to pass that I, Nephi, beheld the power of the Lamb of God, that it descended upon the saints of the church of the Lamb, and upon the covenant people of the Lord, who were scattered upon all the face of the earth; and they were armed with righteousness and with the power of God in great glory.[3]

The time will come when each of us will stand before our Savior and be judged of the deeds done in the flesh. May we remain true to our covenants. May we continue to live in such a way that when the Savior reviews our lives He will smile and say, "THAT'S FAITH!"

---

[2] General Conference, October 1969

[3] 1 Nephi 14:14

About the Author

TIMOTHY L CARVER was employed 37 years as a teacher, media and curriculum writer for The Church of Jesus Christ of Latter-day Saints.

His church callings include serving as bishop, counselor in the stake presidency and high council.

Tim has been happily married for more than 40 years. He has two children and six grandchildren. He enjoys being with family and friends, golfing and riding camels.

Other books by Tim:

- **The Me Monster** – This is a children's book about Jack, a selfish boy who never thinks of anyone but himself. Everyone has given up on Jack. Except his parents, who find a special way to show Jack the terrible monster that is living inside him!

- ***The Super Simple Home Buyer's Handbook*** – This is a collection of our very best home buying tips. And we added the most helpful resources we knew. Then we condensed and simplified them into a short but powerful resource. Quick to read. Easy to understand.

You can find out more about Tim's other books by visiting his website:

www.TimothyLCarver.com

He can also be reached at tlcarver@comcast.net

Did you enjoy this book?

If so, the author would deeply appreciate your kind review on Amazon.

Many thanks!

Printed in Great Britain
by Amazon

74584697R00088